BAHÁ'Í BASICS

BAHÁ'Í BASICS

A GUIDE TO THE BELIEFS, PRACTICES, AND HISTORY OF THE BAHÁ'Í FAITH

FRANCES WORTHINGTON

BAHÁ'Í
PUBLISHING

WILMETTE, ILLINOIS

Bahá'í Publishing
1233 Central St., Evanston, Illinois 60201
Copyright © 2012, 2020 by the National Spiritual Assembly
of the Bahá'ís of the United States

26   25   24   23   7   6   5   4

Library of Congress Cataloging-in-Publication Data

Worthington, Frances.
  Bahá'í Basics : A Guide to the Beliefs, Practices, and History of the Bahá'í Faith / By
Frances Worthington.
      pages cm
  Includes bibliographical references.
  ISBN 978-1-61851-017-4 (pbk. : alk. paper) 1. Bahai Faith. I. Title.
  BP365.W67 2012
  297.9'3—dc23

                                                            2012019787

Cover design by Andrew Johnson
Book design by Patrick Falso

Contents

Preface

This book was written to help answer some of the questions people commonly ask as they begin to study the Bahá'í Faith. Topics range from correct pronunciations, to things as mystical as life after death, and as practical as administration. Quotations from the Bahá'í writings are used plentifully to help minimize my own biases, though admittedly the very process of forming questions and choosing responses is an interpretive act. When a passage is plucked from a full page of sacred scripture and set down to be read in isolation, it runs the risk of being misleading and / or incomplete. For that, the author apologizes in advance.

On the following pages are a few advisories regarding sources, spellings, and pronunciations.

Sources

Although this book contains information from various sources, including the author's own words, the most important words are those in the quotations that have been taken from authoritative Bahá'í writings, which consist of:

- **The sacred writings of the Báb and Bahá'u'lláh**
- **The writings of 'Abdu'l-Bahá**
- **The writings of Shoghi Effendi**, including letters written on his behalf and approved by him.
- **The writings of the Universal House of Justice**, including letters and documents written, with approval, and on its behalf. As the House of Justice has noted, "Unity of doctrine is maintained by the existence of the authentic texts of Scripture and the voluminous interpretations of 'Abdu'l-Bahá and Shoghi Effendi together with the absolute prohibition against anyone propounding 'authoritative' or 'inspired'

interpretations or usurping the function of Guardian. Unity of administration is assured by the authority of the Universal House of Justice." The Universal House of Justice, *Messages from the Universal House of Justice, 1963–1986,* no. 23.20.

It is important to note that some of the quotations in this book are taken from talks given by 'Abdu'l-Bahá. These talks, though a valuable source of information and insight, are not considered authoritative texts nor are they Bahá'í scripture. This includes all quotes from *Paris Talks, The Promulgation of Universal Peace,* and *'Abdu'l-Bahá in London.*

Spellings

Many of the original translations of the words of the Báb, Bahá'u'lláh, and 'Abdu'l-Bahá were made in formal British English. British spelling was used by Shoghi Effendi and continues to be employed by the Universal House of Justice. This accounts for some of the inconsistent spellings (such as *centre and tranquillity),* appearing in quotations, that vary from common American English.

Pronunciations

The pronunciations below are an attempt to represent the way most American Bahá'ís say things—which is not necessarily how someone fluent in Persian or Arabic might pronounce them.

- Pronounce "oo" like the middle of *noon*
- Pronounce "ee" like the middle of *deep*
- CAPITAL LETTERS indicate the syllable(s) that are most often accented

- 'Abdu'l-Bahá (AB-dool-bah-HA)
- Alláh-u-Abhá (ah-LA-hoo-wab-ha)
- Ayyám-i-Há (ah-YAH-mee-ha)
- Báb (bob)
- Bahá (bah-HA)
- Bahá'í (ba-HI)
- Bahá'u'lláh (bah-HA-oo-LA)
- Naw-Rúz (NAW-rooz)
- Riḍván (RIZ-van)
- Shoghi Effendi (SHOW-ghee eh-FEN-dee) Pronounce the "g" like the first letter of *get.*
- Yá-Bahá'u'l-Abhá (YAH-bah-HA-ool-ab-HA)

CHAPTER 1

Who Are the Bahá'ís?

What is the Bahá'í Faith?

The Bahá'í Faith is a religion whose central purpose is establishing the oneness of humanity. Its focus on unity is reflected in the faces of its adherents: Bahá'ís come from virtually every tribe, race, and nationality in the world.

Bahá'ís believe in one God, Who has created the universe and all that dwell therein. God has, with abundant grace, provided spiritual and moral guidance to mankind through a series of divine Messengers—including Moses, Buddha, Christ, and Muḥammad. The Bahá'í Faith was founded in 1863 by Bahá'u'lláh, Whom Bahá'ís accept as the most recent Messenger of God. Bahá'u'lláh's name means "The Glory of God."

How many Bahá'ís are there and where do they live?

Statistics on religious affiliation are difficult to gather and verify, but a conservative estimate of the number of Bahá'ís as of 2020 would be at least five million. Bahá'ís live in more than 100,000 localities around the world and represent more than 2,100 ethnic and tribal groups. The Bahá'í writings have been translated into more than 800 languages.

Do people become Bahá'ís by birth or by choice?

Becoming a Baha'i is a choice. Bahá'ís believe in independent investigation of truth, which means that each person is responsible for learning about religion and deciding what is true. A child born to Bahá'í parents is considered a Bahá'í while young and educated in it tenets, but at age fifteen one is considered spiritually mature and assumes responsibility for affirming one's faith independently. This is explained more fully in chapter 22.

How can different religions of the world be from the same God?

One way to understand the religions of the world is to see them as parts of a single educational system—a school dedicated to increasing mankind's spiritual understanding. There is only one superintendent of this school, but the name you use for Him—Jehovah, Yahweh, Ahura Mazda, Allah, Indra, or God—will depend on the language you speak.

Down through the centuries God has created a number of classrooms and assigned each one its own teacher, known to His followers as a Prophet / Messiah / Manifestation / Messenger. The message of each teacher has been given in a manner suited to the comprehension levels and social skills of the students, which means

that there have been some differences. These differences, however, were never intended to be used as excuses for division or hatred. When religions clash with each other, it is as ridiculous as two children quarreling over whether the truest form of water is ice, snow, sleet, fog, rain, or steam.

Do Bahá'ís have a Bible or a sacred text?

Yes. Bahá'u'lláh wrote in His own hand (and sometimes dictated to a secretary) the texts that Bahá'ís use. The original texts of all of these are stored in the Bahá'í Archives in Haifa, Israel. Bahá'ís also refer to the writings of Bahá'u'lláh's son, 'Abdu'l-Bahá, and His great-grandson, Shoghi Effendi. Learn more about them in chapters 10 and 11.

When and where do Bahá'ís worship?

Bahá'ís can pray and meditate whenever they wish, but there is also a regular community worship service. It is held once every nineteen days, which corresponds to the beginning of each Bahá'í month. In small communities, Bahá'ís meet in each other's homes. Larger communities often buy a building to use as a Bahá'í Center. Chapter 15 deals with the Bahá'í calendar as well as the worship service.

Why is service a common part of Bahá'í life?

Throughout Bahá'í scripture, there are repeated references to the importance of being of service to humanity. "Blessed and happy," Bahá'u'lláh wrote, "is he that ariseth to promote the best interests of the peoples and kindreds of the earth." He also declared that "Man's merit lieth in service and virtue and not in the pageantry of wealth and riches." Bahá'u'lláh, *Gleanings from the Writings of Bahá'u'lláh,* no. 117.1; Baha'u'llah, *Tablets of Bahá'u'lláh,* p. 138.

What types of service activities are Bahá'ís involved in?

Bahá'ís involve themselves in any number of activities that vary according to the needs of their neighborhoods and towns. Individuals may decide, for example, to join an interfaith forum, read to children at a nursery school, serve in a soup kitchen, participate in a recycling initiative, volunteer at a health screening session, etc. But as a group, Bahá'ís are also involved in activities that enhance the spiritual strength and capacity of their neighborhoods. They do this to serve both individuals and the greater community at large.

"The activities that drive this process [the betterment of communities], and in which newly found friends are invited to engage—meetings that strengthen the devotional character of the community; classes that nurture the tender hearts and minds of children; groups that channel the surging energies of junior youth; circles of study, open to all, that enable people of varied backgrounds to advance on equal footing and explore the application of the teachings to their individual and collective lives . . ." The Universal House of Justice, Riḍván Message, 2010.

How are Bahá'ís organized? Is there a clergy?

The Bahá'í Faith does not have any ministers, rabbis, or clergy. Instead, Bahá'ís form governing bodies through elections. Local Spiritual Assemblies administer the affairs of individual communities, National Spiritual Assemblies cover a nation, and the Universal House of Justice is the final authority for the world. Details of the administrative order are in chapter 13.

Do Bahá'ís believe in life after death?

Yes. From a Bahá'í perspective, when the body dies, the soul is released from its attachment to this world and enters the world of the spirit, which is vastly different from physical life. In this material world we need a physical body with fingers and toes, eyes and ears. In the next world—the world after death—the soul is in need of spiritual qualities like justice, love, and honesty if it is to function well.

Are we judged after death?
What about heaven and hell?

Our actions in this world will, Bahá'u'lláh promises, be judged at the moment of death and receive a recompense according to the estimate of God. Hell, Bahá'u'lláh explains, is remoteness from God. Heaven is nearness to Him. Read more about this in chapter 3.

Why was there a need for a new Messenger? Why did Bahá'u'lláh come?

There are natural cycles to all things, including religion. God has ordained a beginning, a middle, and an end to each religious cycle and has given each a special purpose.

A religious cycle starts with a period that we can call the divine springtime. This is when a Messenger of God announces His mission and begins to attract followers. At first it is very difficult for the new faith to attract adherents. People either ignore it or object to it and persecute its believers. As spring moves along, however, larger numbers of people begin to follow the new Messenger and put His teachings into practice. This has a transforming effect on the whole society.

The summer of a religion is when its true purpose can be seen in the fruits of a great civilization. Every facet of life reflects the influence of the Messenger.

In autumn, chilly winds begin to blow. Mankind becomes less obedient to the teachings and obscures their true meanings with superstition and tradition.

By the time fall has given way to winter, nearly every trace of spirituality has been buried under blizzards of hatred, materialism, and manmade dogma. Only the coming of a new Messenger, like the shining of the spring sun, can thaw icy hearts and coax them into blooming.

At our current place in human history, the world stands in need of help. The advance of scientific knowledge along with rapid travel and instant communication has dissolved the borders of every country and introduced possibilities for global catastrophes unimaginable in the past. We know that for the sake of our children and grandchildren, things must change, but we don't have consensus on how to start. We are spiritually frozen.

Bahá'u'lláh has been sent by God to provide the divine assistance we need. His revelation has inaugurated a new spiritual cycle that holds within it the promise of universal peace. We are in the earliest part of the spring of that cycle, beset by periodic frosts that fool us into thinking that things will never get better. But, Bahá'u'lláh assures us, we should not despair. God has destined that the hours of sunlight will gradually increase. The days will assuredly grow warmer. Spiritual summer will come.

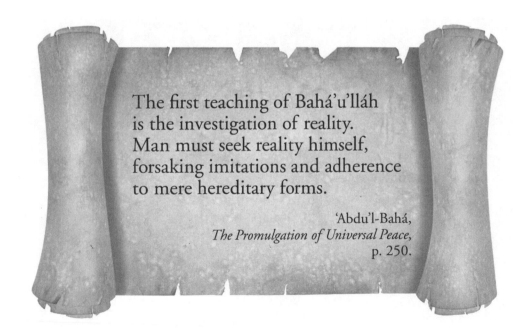

The first teaching of Bahá'u'lláh is the investigation of reality. Man must seek reality himself, forsaking imitations and adherence to mere hereditary forms.

'Abdu'l-Bahá,
The Promulgation of Universal Peace,
p. 250.

CHAPTER 2

The Purpose of Creation

God, Physical and Spiritual Life, the Nature of the Soul

"All praise to the unity of God, and all honor to Him, the sovereign Lord, the incomparable and all-glorious Ruler of the universe, Who, out of utter nothingness, hath created the reality of all things, Who, from naught, hath brought into being the most refined and subtle elements of His creation. . . ." Bahá'u'lláh, *Gleanings from the Writings of Bahá'u'lláh,* no. 27.1.

Who is the Creator?

"No God is there but Thee, the All-Possessing, the Most Exalted. Thou art He Who createth from naught the universe and all that dwell therein." The Báb, *Selections from the Writings of the Báb,* no. 7:32:1.

Why did God create us?

O Son of Man! Veiled in My immemorial being and in the ancient eternity of My essence, I knew My love for thee; therefore I created thee, have engraved on thee Mine image and revealed to thee My beauty.

Bahá'u'lláh,
Hidden Words, Arabic, no. 3.

Can we understand God?

We can never fully understand God because the created cannot comprehend the Creator. We can, however, learn about God through His Messengers (described below as "Daystars" of divine guidance), and we can appreciate the traces of God found throughout His creation:

"No man's understanding shall ever gain access unto His holy, court. As a token of His mercy, however, and as a proof of His loving-kindness, He hath manifested unto men the Daystars of His divine guidance, the Symbols of His divine unity, and hath ordained the knowledge of these sanctified Beings to be identical with the knowledge of His own Self." Bahá'u'lláh, *Gleanings from the Writings of Bahá'u'lláh*, no. 21.1.

"How shall we know God? We know Him by His attributes. We know Him by His signs. We know Him by His names. We know not what the reality of the sun is, but we know the sun by the ray, by the heat, by its efficacy and penetration. We recognize the sun by its bounty and effulgence, but as to what constitutes the reality of the solar energy, that is unknowable to us. The attributes characterizing the sun, however, are knowable. If we wish to come in touch with the reality of Divinity, we do so by recognizing its phenomena, its attributes and traces, which are widespread in the universe." 'Abdu'l-Bahá, *The Promulgation of Universal Peace*, p. 595.

Did creation have a beginning? Will it ever end?

"The one true God hath everlastingly existed, and will everlastingly continue to exist. His creation, likewise, hath had no beginning, and will have no end." Bahá'u'lláh, *Gleanings from the Writings of Bahá'u'lláh*, no. 82.10.

What is the purpose of creation?

Man's capacity to know and love God is the primary purpose of creation:

"Having created the world and all that liveth and moveth therein, He, through the direct operation of His unconstrained and sovereign Will, chose to confer upon man the unique distinction and capacity to know Him and to love Him—a capacity that must needs be regarded as the generating impulse and the primary purpose underlying the whole of creation." Bahá'u'lláh, *Gleanings from the Writings of Bahá'u'lláh*, no. 27.2.

What is the connection between God and nature?

Nature is a physical expression of the will of God, and each part of the natural world can be understood as reflecting one of His attributes:

"Nature is in its essence the embodiment of My Name, the Maker, the Creator." Bahá'u'lláh, *Tablets of Bahá'u'lláh,* p. 142.

"Upon the inmost reality of each and every created thing He hath shed the light of one of His names, and made it a recipient of the glory of one of His attributes." Bahá'u'lláh, *Gleanings from the Writings of Bahá'u'lláh,* no. 27.2.

Is the physical world the real world?

Although the physical world is fascinating and wonderful, when it is compared to the Kingdom of God, it is as insubstantial as a shadow:

"The world is but a show, vain and empty, a mere nothing, bearing the semblance of reality. Set not your affections upon it. . . . Verily I say, the world is like the vapor in a desert, which the thirsty dreameth to be water and striveth after it with all his might, until when he cometh unto it, he findeth it to be mere illusion." Bahá'u'lláh, *Gleanings from the Writings of Bahá'u'lláh,* no. 153.8.

"Know thou that the Kingdom is the real world, and this nether place is only its shadow stretching out. A shadow hath no life of its own; its existence is only a fantasy, and nothing more; it is but images reflected in water, and seeming as pictures to the eye." 'Abdu'l-Bahá, *Selections from the Writings of 'Abdu'l-Bahá,* no. 150.2.

What is true life?

The life of the spirit is the life for which we were created:

"Wert thou to attain to but a dewdrop of the crystal waters of divine knowledge, thou wouldst readily realize that true life is not the life of the flesh but the life of the spirit. For the life of the flesh is common to both men and animals, whereas the life of the spirit is possessed only by the pure in heart who have quaffed from the ocean of faith and partaken of the fruit of certitude. This life knoweth no death, and this existence is crowned by immortality." Bahá'u'lláh, Kitáb-i-Íqán, ¶128.

What is the difference between the life of the body and the life of the spirit?

One way to compare these things is to think about the existence of a stone as compared to the existence of a person. A stone exists, but its life is very limited compared to the life of a person. And the life of a person who concentrates only on his body is much more limited than that of a person who also develops his spirit:

"Life is of two kinds: that of the body and that of the spirit. The life of the body is material life, but the life of the spirit expresses the existence of the Kingdom, which consists in receiving the Spirit of God and becoming vivified by the breath of the Holy Spirit. Although the material life has existence, it is pure nonexistence and absolute death for the holy saints. So man exists, and this stone also exists, but what a difference between the existence of man and that of the stone! Though the stone exists, in relation to the existence of man it is nonexistent." 'Abdu'l-Bahá, *Some Answered Questions,* pp. 241–42.

How is physical life a tool for understanding spiritual life?

"The spiritual world is like unto the phenomenal world. They are the exact counterpart of each other. Whatever objects appear in this world of existence are the outer pictures of the world of heaven." 'Abdu'l-Bahá, *The Promulgation of Universal Peace,* p. 12.

The Effect of Spiritual Development

Does spiritual development affect the physical world?

"The chief reason for the evils now rampant in society is the lack of spirituality. The materialistic civilization of our age has so much absorbed the energy and interest of mankind that people in general no longer feel the necessity of raising themselves above the forces and conditions of their daily material existence. There is not sufficient demand for things that we should call spiritual to differentiate them from the needs and requirements of our physical existence. The universal crisis affecting mankind is, therefore, essentially spiritual in its causes. The spirit of the age, taken on the whole, is irreligious. Man's outlook on life is too crude and materialistic to enable him to elevate himself into the higher realms of the spirit." Shoghi Effendi, cited in *Messages from the Universal House of Justice, 1963–1986,* no. 397.2c.

What about the environment?

The environment directly reflects our hearts, which means that we cannot expect to improve it without also improving the quality of our inner lives:

"We cannot segregate the human heart from the environment outside us and say that once one of these is reformed everything will be improved. Man is organic with the world. His inner life moulds the environment and is itself deeply affected by it. The one acts upon the other and every abiding change in the life of man is the result of these mutual reactions." Letter written on behalf of Shoghi Effendi, in *Compilation of Compilations, vol. I,* p. 84.

Which is more important, spiritual or physical development?

For the sake of the world and for the sake of our souls, we need a balance between them, just as a bird relies on two wings of equal strength:

"Man has two powers; and his development, two aspects. One power is connected with the material world, and by it he is capable of material advancement. The other power is spiritual, and through its development his inner, poten-

tial nature is awakened. These powers are like two wings. Both must be developed, for flight is impossible with one wing. Praise be to God! Material advancement has been evident in the world, but there is need of spiritual advancement in like proportion. We must strive unceasingly and without rest to accomplish the development of the spiritual nature in man, and endeavor with tireless energy to advance humanity toward the nobility of its true and intended station." 'Abdu'l-Bahá, *The Promulgation of Universal Peace,* p. 81.

How can people be happy?

A balance between material and spiritual progress is necessary to establish the happiness of the world:

"No matter how far the material world advances, it cannot establish the happiness of mankind. Only when material and spiritual civilization are linked and coordinated will happiness be assured. Then material civilization will not contribute its energies to the force of evil in destroying the oneness of humanity, for in material civilization good and evil advance together and maintain the same pace." 'Abdu'l-Bahá, *The Promulgation of Universal Peace,* p. 151.

The Nature of the Soul

The soul of man is the sun by which his body is illumined, and from which it draweth its sustenance . . .

Bahá'u'lláh,
Gleanings from the Writings of Bahá'u'lláh, no. 80.4.

What is the soul?

The nature of the soul is mysterious. If it is faithful to God, it will reflect His light:

"Verily I say, the human soul is, in its essence, one of the signs of God, a mystery among His mysteries. It is one of the mighty signs of God. Within it lieth concealed that which the world is now utterly incapable of apprehending." Bahá'u'lláh, *Gleanings from the Writings of Bahá'u'lláh,* no. 82.6.

"Thou hast asked Me concerning the nature of the soul. Know, verily, that the soul is a sign of God, a heavenly gem whose reality the most learned of men hath failed to grasp, and whose mystery no mind, however acute, can ever hope to unravel. It is the first among all created things to declare the excellence of its Creator, the first to recognize His glory, to cleave to His truth, and to bow down in adoration before Him. If it be faithful to God, it will reflect His light, and will, eventually, return unto Him. If it fail, however, in its allegiance to its Creator, it will become a victim to self and passion, and will, in the end, sink in their depths." Bahá'u'lláh, *Gleanings from the Writings of Bahá'u'lláh,* no. 82.1.

How are the soul and body connected?

"The connection of the spirit with the body is like that of the sun with the mirror. . . . Therefore, it is evident and certain that the spirit is different from the body, and that its duration is independent of that of the body; on the contrary, the spirit with the utmost greatness rules in the world of the body; and its power and influence, like the bounty of the sun in the mirror, are apparent and visible. But when the mirror becomes dusty or breaks, it will cease to reflect the rays of the sun." 'Abdu'l-Bahá, *Some Answered Questions,* p. 229.

Is the soul affected when a person is sick or mentally ill?

No, the soul is not affected by what happens to the body:

"Know thou that the soul of man is exalted above, and is independent of all infirmities of body or mind. That a sick person showeth signs of weakness is due to the hindrances that interpose themselves between his soul and his body, for the soul itself remaineth unaffected by any bodily ailments . . . every malady afflicting the body of man is an impediment that preventeth the soul from manifesting its inherent might and power. When it leaveth the body, however, it will evince such ascendancy, and reveal such influence as no force on earth can equal." Bahá'u'lláh, *Gleanings from the Writings of Bahá'u'lláh,* no. 80.2.

When does a soul begin its life?

"The soul of man comes into being at conception." Shoghi Effendi, in *Lights of Guidance,* no. 1820.

How long does a soul live?

"The soul is not a combination of elements, it is not composed of many atoms, it is of one indivisible substance and therefore eternal. It is entirely out of the order of the physical creation; it is immortal!" 'Abdu'l-Bahá, *Paris Talks,* no. 29.13.

My eternity is My creation,
I have created it for thee.
Bahá'u'lláh, Hidden Words,
Arabic, no. 64.

Can the soul be affected by something while a person is asleep?

"When man is asleep, his soul can, in no wise, be said to have been inherently affected by any external object." Bahá'u'lláh, *Gleanings from the Writings of Bahá'u'lláh,* no. 82.4.

Do animals have souls?

"Even the most developed dog has not the immortal soul of the man; yet the dog is perfect in its own place. You do not quarrel with a rose-tree because it cannot sing!" 'Abdu'l-Bahá, *'Abdu'l-Bahá in London,* p. 97.

CHAPTER 3

The Life of the Soul

Life After Death, Judgment, Heaven and Hell

O SON OF THE SUPREME! I have made death a messenger of joy to thee. Wherefore dost thou grieve? I made the light to shed on thee its splendor. Why dost thou veil thyself therefrom?

Bahá'u'lláh,
Hidden Words, Arabic,
no. 32.

What is it like when we die and our souls enter the next world?

Although each soul begins its path of growth and development through association with a physical body, its ultimate home lies within the eternal kingdom of God. In the Bahá'í writings, the growth and development of a person's soul is compared to the growth and development of a baby in its mother's womb. Before it is born, the baby has no need of the eyes and mouth and feet that it is developing because it cannot see, speak, or walk yet. If you tried to explain to the baby how important these things would be, it would not be able to understand.

> . . . in the other world the human reality doth not assume a physical form, rather doth it take on a heavenly form, made up of elements of that heavenly realm.
>
> 'Abdu'l-Bahá,
> *Selections from the Writings of 'Abdu'l-Bahá,* no. 163.5.

While our body is alive, our soul has the chance to develop its capacity for spiritual qualities like truth, justice, and love. When the soul is released from its connection to the body by death, these spiritual qualities will function much like our hands, eyes, and ears functioned in this world. Like the unborn baby, however, we find it impossible to imagine exactly what the life after this one will be like.

What does a soul look like in the next world?

"The nature of the soul after death can never be described, nor is it meet and permissible to reveal its whole character to the eyes of men. The Prophets and Messengers of God have been sent down for the sole purpose of guid-ing mankind to the straight Path of Truth. The purpose underlying Their revelation hath been to educate all men, that they may, at the hour of death, ascend, in the utmost purity and sanctity and with absolute detachment, to the throne of the Most High." Bahá'u'lláh, *Gleanings from the Writings of Bahá'u'lláh,* no. 81.1.

Does a soul continue to make spiritual progress after death?

Yes, spiritual progress is the natural state of the soul:

"Know thou of a truth that the soul, after its separation from the body, will continue to progress until it attaineth the presence of God, in a state and condition which neither the revolution of ages and centuries, nor the changes and chances of this world, can alter." Bahá'u'lláh, *Gleanings from the Writings of Bahá'u'lláh,* no. 81.1.

"As to the soul of man after death, it remains in the degree of purity to which it has evolved during life in the physical body, and after it is freed from the body it remains plunged in the ocean of God's Mercy.

"From the moment the soul leaves the body and arrives in the Heavenly World, its evolution is spiritual, and that evolution is: *The approaching unto God.*" 'Abdu'l-Bahá, *Paris Talks,* no. 20.12–13.

What about suicide?

Suicide is forbidden and has a negative effect on the soul:

"God, who is the Author of all life can alone take it away, and dispose of it in a way He deems best. Whoever commits suicide endangers his soul, and will suffer spiritually as a result. . ." Shoghi Effendi, *Messages to Canada,* pp. 66–67.

Will we recognize the souls of other people in the next world?

"According to Bahá'u'lláh, the soul retains its individuality and consciousness after death, and is able to commune with other souls. This communion, however, is purely spiritual in character, and is conditioned upon the disinterested and selfless love of the individuals for each other." Letter written on behalf of Shoghi Effendi, in *Lights of Guidance,* no. 694.

What qualities are needed by the soul in the next world?

"What is he in need of in the Kingdom which transcends the life and limitation of this mortal sphere? That world beyond is a world of sanctity and radiance; therefore, it is necessary that in this world he should acquire these divine attributes. In that world there is need of spirituality, faith, assurance, the knowledge and love of God. These he must attain in this world so that after his ascension from the earthly to the heavenly Kingdom he shall find all that is needful in that eternal life ready for him.

"That divine world is manifestly a world of lights; therefore, man has need of illumination here. That is a world of love; the love of God is essential. It is a world of perfections; virtues, or perfections, must be acquired. That world is vivified by the breaths of the Holy Spirit; in this world we must seek them. That is the Kingdom of everlasting life; it must be attained during this vanishing existence." 'Abdu'l-Bahá, *The Promulgation of Universal Peace,* p. 316.

What happens to the souls of infants and children who die?

Here are the comforting words addressed by 'Abdu'l-Bahá to a mother who had lost her son:

"O thou beloved maidservant of God, although the loss of a son is indeed heartbreaking and beyond the limits of human endurance, yet one who knoweth and understandeth is assured that the son hath not been lost but, rather, hath stepped from this world into another, and she will find him in the divine realm. That reunion shall be for eternity, while in this world separation is inevitable and bringeth with it a burning grief. . . . Therefore be thou not disconsolate, do not languish, do not sigh, neither wail nor weep; for agitation and mourning deeply affect his soul in the divine realm.

That beloved child addresseth thee from the hidden world: 'O thou kind Mother, thank divine Providence that I have been freed from a small and gloomy cage and, like the birds of the meadows, have soared to the divine world—a world which is spacious, illumined, and ever gay and jubilant. Therefore, lament not, O Mother, and be not grieved; I am not of the lost, nor have I been obliterated and destroyed. I have shaken off the mortal form and have raised my banner in this spiritual world. Following this separation is everlasting companionship. Thou

The souls of children

These children abide under the shadow of the Divine Providence, and, as they have committed no sin and are unsullied by the defilements of the world of nature, they will become the manifestations of divine bounty and the glances of the eye of divine mercy will be directed towards them.

'Abdu'l-Bahá,
Some Answered Questions,
no. 66.8.

shalt find me in the heaven of the Lord, immersed in an ocean of light.'" 'Abdu'l-Bahá, *Selections from the Writings of 'Abdu'l-Bahá*, nos. 171.1–3.

"It is as if a kind gardener transferreth a fresh and tender shrub from a confined place to a wide open area. This transfer is not the cause of the withering, the lessening or the destruction of that shrub; nay, on the contrary, it maketh it to grow and thrive, acquire freshness and delicacy, become green and bear fruit. This hidden secret is well known to the gardener, but those souls who are unaware of this bounty suppose that the gardener, in his anger and wrath, hath uprooted the shrub. Yet to those who are aware,

this concealed fact is manifest, and this predestined decree is considered a bounty. Do not feel grieved or disconsolate, therefore . . ." 'Abdu'l-Bahá, *Selections from the Writings of 'Abdu'l-Bahá*, no. 169.2.

Though death destroy his body, it has no power over his spirit—this is eternal, everlasting, both birthless and deathless.
'Abdu'l-Bahá, *Paris Talks*, no. 20.11.

Eternal Life

What is the meaning of eternal life?

Eternal life is more than the life of the body, and it is more than the mere existence of a soul in the next world. It is a state of spiritual consciousness that opens one's awareness to the gifts of God. Some people describe the experience of becoming aware of eternal life as being born again or as being baptized by the Holy Spirit. Bahá'í scripture compares it to the opening of the petals of a flower that once was nothing more than a hard seed:

"The meaning of eternal life is the gift of the Holy Spirit, as the flower receives the gift of the season, the air, and the breezes of spring. Consider: this flower had life in the beginning like the life of the mineral; but by the coming of the season of spring, of the bounty of the clouds of the springtime, and of the heat of the glowing sun, it attained to another life of the utmost freshness, delicacy and fragrance. The first life of the flower, in comparison to the second life, is death." 'Abdu'l-Bahá, *Some Answered Questions,* p. 242.

Can we experience eternal life and physical life simultaneously?

"Though our bodies be gathered here together, yet our spellbound hearts are carried away by Thy love, and yet are we transported by the rays of Thy resplendent face. Weak though we be, we await the revelations of Thy might and power. Poor though we be, with neither goods nor means, still take we riches from the treasures of Thy Kingdom. Drops though we be, still do we draw from out Thy ocean deeps. Motes though we be, still do we gleam in the glory of Thy splendid Sun." 'Abdu'l-Bahá, *Selections from the Writings of 'Abdu'l-Bahá,* no. 37.5.

How can we acquire the qualities that give us eternal life?

"By what means can man acquire these things? How shall he obtain these merciful gifts and powers? First, through the knowledge of God. Second, through the love of God. Third, through faith. Fourth, through philanthropic deeds. Fifth, through self-sacrifice. Sixth, through severance from this world. Seventh, through sanctity and holiness. Unless he acquires these forces and attains to these requirements, he will surely be deprived of the life that is eternal. But if he possesses the knowledge of God, becomes ignited through the fire of the love of God, witnesses the great and mighty signs of the Kingdom, becomes the cause of love among mankind and lives in the utmost state of sanctity and holiness, he shall surely attain to second birth, be baptized by the Holy Spirit and enjoy everlasting existence." 'Abdu'l-Bahá, *The Promulgation of Universal Peace*, p. 316.

My eternity is My creation, I have created it for thee. Make it the garment of thy temple.
Bahá'u'lláh, Hidden Words,
Arabic, no. 64.

What about reincarnation?

From a Bahá'í perspective, the origin of ideas about reincarnation seems to lie in a misunderstanding of the spiritual teachings of some of the Messengers of God and not from the Messengers themselves. The Bahá'í understanding is that we are born into life on this planet only once and that it is not necessary for us to return

to this planet and be born into another body in order to advance spiritually or grow closer to God.

Judgment in the Afterlife

"Ye, and all ye possess, shall pass away. Ye shall, most certainly, return to God and shall be called to account for your doings in the presence of Him Who shall gather together the entire creation. . . ." Bahá'u'lláh, *Gleanings from the Writings of Bahá'u'lláh*, no. 116.1.

"Bring thyself to account each day ere thou art summoned to a reckoning; for death, unheralded, shall come upon thee and thou shalt be called to give account for thy deeds." Bahá'u'lláh, Hidden Words, Arabic, no. 31.

How will I be judged?

"For every act performed there shall be a recompense according to the estimate of God, and unto this the very ordinances and prohibitions prescribed by the Almighty amply bear witness. For surely if deeds were not rewarded and yielded no fruit, then the Cause of God—exalted is He—would prove futile." Bahá'u'lláh, *Tablets of Bahá'u'lláh*, p. 189.

Heaven and Hell

In Bahá'í scripture, heaven and hell are explained as spiritual states. Heaven is perfection; while hell is imperfection. The beauty of heaven is a spiritual beauty and the ugliness of hell is spiritual degradation. Heaven is nearness to God while hell is remoteness from Him. We can experience heaven or hell while still on this earth, but they are even more clear after death.

"'Where is Paradise, and where is Hell?' Say: 'The one is reunion with Me; the other thine own self . . .'" Bahá'u'lláh, Epistle to the Son of the Wolf, p 132.

". . . just as the effects of the uterine life are not to be found in that dark and narrow place, and only when the child is transferred to this wide earth do the benefits and uses of growth and development in that previous world become revealed—so likewise reward and punishment, heaven and hell, requital and retribution for actions done in this present life, will stand revealed in that other world beyond." 'Abdu'l-Bahá, *Selections from the Writings of 'Abdu'l-Bahá*, no. 156.10.

"The Kingdom [of God] is outwardly referred to as 'heaven,' but this is an expression and likeness and not a factual statement or reality. For the Kingdom is not a material location but is sanctified above time and place. It is a spiritual realm, a divine world, and it is the seat of the sovereignty of the almighty Lord. It is exalted above bodies and all that is corporeal, and it is freed and sanctified from the idle conjectures of men. For to be confined to place is a characteristic of bodies and not of spirits: Time and place encompass the body, not the mind and the soul." 'Abdu'l-Bahá, *Some Answered Questions*, no. 67.1.

O my God! O Thou forgiver of sins, bestower of gifts, dispeller of afflictions!

Verily, I beseech Thee to forgive the sins of such as have abandoned the physical garment and have ascended to the spiritual world.

O my Lord! Purify them from trespasses, dispel their sorrows, and change their darkness into light. Cause them to enter the garden of happiness, cleanse them with the most pure water, and grant them to behold Thy splendors on the loftiest mount.

'Abdu'l-Bahá,
in *Bahá'í Prayers,* p. 41.

CHAPTER 4

Good and Evil

A very simple description of the Bahá'í understanding of good and evil is that good is like light and evil is like the darkness that appears in the absence of light. Just as we must exert physical effort to light a candle to banish the darkness, so we must exert spiritual effort to acquire good qualities that will illumine our souls and banish the shadows of evil.

"Evil is nonexistent; it is the absence of good. Sickness is the loss of health; poverty, the lack of riches. When wealth disappears, you are poor; you look within the treasure box but find nothing there. Without knowledge there is ignorance; therefore, ignorance is simply the lack of knowledge. Death is the absence of life. Therefore, on the one hand, we have existence; on the other, nonexistence, negation or absence of existence." 'Abdu'l-Bahá, *The Promulgation of Universal Peace*, p. 412.

What is the worst of evils?

". . . the worst of all qualities and the most odious of all attributes, and the very foundation of all evil, is lying, and that no more evil or reprehensible quality can be imagined in all existence. It brings all human perfections to naught and gives rise to countless vices. There is no worse attribute than this, and it is the foundation of all wickedness." 'Abdu'l-Bahá, *Some Answered Questions,* no. 57.12.

Why does evil exist?

We often wonder why God created us with the potential for both good and evil because we think we would be happier in a world without evil and without suffering. However, Bahá'í scripture explains that a world without the potential for evil would be a world without free will. We couldn't choose to do good or evil because everything would be good. And we wouldn't be able to experience the bliss of spiritual growth because we would already be perfect.

God Himself does not compel the soul to become spiritual. The exercise of the free human will is necessary. 'Abdu'l-Bahá, cited in Esslemont, *Bahá'u'lláh and the New Era,* p. 145.

. . . the journey of the soul is necessary. The pathway of life is the road which leads to divine knowledge and attainment. 'Abdu'l-Bahá, *The Promulgation of Universal Peace,* p. 412.

"Man must walk in many paths and be subjected to various processes in his evolution upward. Physically he is not born in full stature but passes through consecutive stages of fetus, infant, childhood, youth, maturity and old age. Suppose he had the power to remain young throughout his life. He then would not understand the meaning of old age and could not believe it existed. If he could not realize the condition of old age, he would not know that he was young. He would not know the difference between young and old without experiencing the old. Unless you have passed through the state of infancy, how would you know this was an infant beside you? If there were no wrong, how would you recognize the right? If it were not for sin, how would you appreciate virtue? If evil deeds were unknown, how could you commend good actions? If sickness did not exist, how would you understand health?" 'Abdu'l-Bahá, *The Promulgation of Universal Peace,* p. 412.

Goodness in Everything

"Noble have I created thee, yet thou hast abased thyself. Rise then unto that for which thou wast created." Bahá'u'lláh, Hidden Words, Arabic, no. 22.

In spite of all the descriptions of good and evil existing in the nature of each person, Bahá'í scripture points out that when the qualities we possess are carefully examined, all of them are potentially good. Nothing in God's creation is inherently evil. Man is essentially noble and every trait—even greed—can be harnessed and used for a praiseworthy purpose:

"In the innate nature of things there is no evil—all is good. This applies even to certain apparently blameworthy attributes and dispositions which seem inherent in some people, but which are not in reality reprehensible. For example, you can see in a nursing child, from the beginning of its life, the signs of greed, of anger, and of ill temper; and so it might be argued that good and evil are innate in the reality of man, and that this is contrary to the pure goodness of the innate nature and of creation. The answer is that greed, which is to demand ever more, is a praiseworthy quality provided that it is displayed under the right circumstances. Thus, should a person show greed in acquiring science and knowledge, or in the exercise of compassion, high-mindedness, and justice, this would be most praiseworthy. And should he direct his anger and wrath against the bloodthirsty tyrants who are like ferocious beasts, this too would be most praiseworthy. But should he display these qualities under other conditions, this would be deserving of blame." 'Abdu'l-Bahá, *Some Answered Questions*, no. 57.10.

The Existence of Satan

One way to understand the Bahá'í concept of Satan as the symbol of evil is to think about how love is symbolized by a winged cherub carrying a bow and arrow. The force of love is real and can be expressed through loving acts even though it is not a physical entity. Indeed, we may say we have been shot by the arrow of love even though no cherub has flown in the window and no shaft has pierced our skin. In much the same way, we can speak of an evil act being inspired by the devil and can suffer from the effects of that act even though it did not involve a tangible creature wielding a pitchfork.

Do evil spirits exist?

". . . the evil spirit, Satan or whatever is interpreted as evil, refers to the lower nature in man. This baser nature is symbolized in various ways . . . God has never created an evil spirit; all such ideas and nomenclature are symbols expressing the mere human or earthly nature of man." 'Abdu'l-Bahá, *The Promulgation of Universal Peace*, p. 411.

"The attributes of God are love and mercy; the attribute of Satan is hate. Therefore, he who is merciful and kind to his fellowmen is manifesting the divine attribute, and he who is hating and hostile toward a fellow creature is satanic. God is absolute love, even as Jesus Christ has declared, and Satan is utter hatred. Wherever love is witnessed, know that there is a manifestation of God's mercy; whenever you meet hatred and enmity, know that these are the evidences and attributes of Satan." 'Abdu'l-Bahá, *The Promulgation of Universal Peace*, pp. 54–55.

Are some people owned by Satan or does everyone belong to God?

". . . all mankind are the servants of one God; God is the Father of all; there is not a single exception to that law. There are no people of Satan; all belong to the Merciful. There is no darkness; all is light. All are the servants of God, and man must love humanity from his heart. He must, verily, behold humanity as submerged in the divine mercy." 'Abdu'l-Bahá, *The Promulgation of Universal Peace*, p. 372.

This lower nature in man is symbolized as Satan—the evil ego within us, not an evil personality outside.
'Abdu'l-Bahá, *The Promulgation of Universal Peace*, p. 400.

The Satanic Ego

Should we strive to subdue our satanic egos?

"Follow not that which the Evil One whispereth in your hearts, for he, verily, doth prompt you to walk after your lusts and covetous desires, and hindereth you from treading the straight Path." Bahá'u'lláh, *The Summons of the Lord of Hosts,* ¶ 98.

". . . the ego, the dark, animalistic heritage each one of us has, the lower nature that can develop into a monster of selfishness, brutality, lust and so on. It is this self we must struggle against, or this side of our natures, in order to strengthen and free the spirit within us and help it to attain perfection." Letter written on behalf of Shoghi Effendi, *Messages to Canada,* p. 99.

Why is life so hard?

"Effort is an inseparable part of man's life. It may take different forms with the changing conditions of the world, but it will be always present as a necessary element in our earthly existence. Life is after all a struggle. Progress is attained through struggle, and without such a struggle life ceases to have a meaning; it becomes even extinct." Letter written on behalf of Shoghi Effendi, in *Lights of Guidance,* no. 1870.

"The incomparable Creator hath created all men from one same substance, and hath exalted their reality above the rest of His creatures. Success or failure, gain or loss, must, therefore, depend upon man's own exertions. The more he striveth, the greater will be his progress." Bahá'u'lláh, *Gleanings from the Writings of Bahá'u'lláh,* no. 34.8.

If everything is potentially good, why is there so much trouble in the world?

"Indeed the actions of man himself breed a profusion of satanic power. For were men to abide by and observe the divine teachings, every trace of evil would be banished from the face of the earth. However, the widespread differences that exist among mankind and the prevalence of sedition, contention, conflict and the like are the primary factors which provoke the appearance of the satanic spirit. Yet the Holy Spirit hath ever shunned such matters. A world in which naught can be perceived save strife, quarrels and corruption is bound to become the seat of the throne, the very metropolis, of Satan." Bahá'u'lláh, *Tablets of Baha'u'lláh,* pp. 176–77.

"Lauded and glorified art thou, O my God! I entreat Thee by the sighing of Thy lovers and by the tears shed by them that long to behold Thee, not to withhold from me Thy tender mercies in Thy Day, nor to deprive me of the melodies of the Dove that extolleth Thy oneness before the light that shineth from thy face. I am the one who is in misery, O God! Behold me cleaving fast to Thy Name, the All-Possessing. I am the one who is sure to perish; behold me clinging to Thy Name, the Imperishable. I implore Thee, therefore, by Thy Self, the Exalted, the Most High, not to abandon me unto mine own self and unto the desires of a corrupt inclination. Hold Thou my hand with the hand of Thy power, and deliver me from the depths of my fancies and idle imaginings, and cleanse me of all that is abhorrent unto Thee.

Cause me, then, to turn wholly unto Thee, to put my whole trust in Thee, to seek Thee as my Refuge, and to flee unto Thy face. Thou art, verily, He Who, through the power of His might, doeth whatsoever He desireth, and commandeth, through the potency of His will, whatsoever He chooseth. None can withstand the operation of Thy decree; none can divert the course of Thine appointment. Thou art, in truth, the Almighty, the All-Glorious, the Most Bountiful." Bahá'u'lláh, in *Bahá'í Prayers,* pp. 224–25.

[P]eace is from God while warfare is satanic. Man must emulate the merciful God and turn away from satanic promptings in order that universal inclination shall be toward peace, love and unity and the discord of war vanish.

'Abdu'l-Bahá, *The Promulgation of Universal Peace,* p. 325.

CHAPTER 5

Continuing Revelation

God and His Messengers

How has religious truth been progressively revealed?

"The fundamental principle enunciated by Bahá'u'lláh . . . is that religious truth is not absolute but relative, that Divine Revelation is a continuous and progressive process, that all the great religions of the world are divine in origin, that their basic principles are in complete harmony, that their aims and purposes are one and the same, that their teachings are but facets of one truth, that their functions are complementary, that they differ only in the nonessential aspects of their doctrines, and that their missions represent successive stages in the spiritual

The reality of Divinity is like an endless ocean. Revelation may be likened to the rain. Can you imagine the cessation of rain?

'Abdu'l-Bahá, *The Promulgation of Universal Peace,* p. 533.

evolution of human society." Shoghi Effendi, *The Promised Day Is Come*, ¶i.

Will God ever stop revealing Himself?

"Among the bounties of God is revelation. Hence revelation is progressive and continuous. It never ceases. It is necessary that the reality of Divinity with all its perfections and attributes should become resplendent in the human world." 'Abdu'l-Bahá, *The Promulgation of Universal Peace*, p. 533.

What has been the purpose of the Messengers of God?

Each divine Messenger brings a revelation that is suited to a certain time and place. Each provides spiritual education and fosters the establishment of a peaceful existence:

"Every Prophet Whom the Almighty and Peerless Creator hath purposed to send to the peoples of the earth hath been entrusted with a Message, and charged to act in a manner that would best meet the requirements of the age in which He appeared. God's purpose in sending His Prophets unto men is twofold. The first is to liberate the children of men from the darkness of ignorance, and guide them to the light of true understanding. The second is to ensure the peace and tranquillity of mankind, and provide all

the means by which they can be established." Bahá'u'lláh, *Gleanings from the Writings of Bahá'u'lláh*, no. 34.5.

What are the differences among the Messengers of God?

The Messengers are all absolutely alike in having been sent by God to mankind as His representatives on earth, and They deserve equal honor and respect. They are different because each one has a specific revelation, a distinct personality, and acts in ways suited to the people of the era in which They appear:

"Know thou assuredly that the essence of all the Prophets of God is one and the same. Their unity is absolute. God, the Creator, saith: There is no distinction whatsoever among the Bearers of My Message. They all have but one purpose; their secret is the same secret. To prefer one in honor to another, to exalt certain ones above the rest, is in no wise to be permitted. . . The measure of the revelation of the Prophets of God in this world, however, must differ. Each and every one of them hath been the Bearer of a distinct Message, and hath been commissioned to reveal Himself through specific acts. It is for this reason that they appear to vary in their greatness." Bahá'u'lláh, *Gleanings from the Writings of Bahá'u'lláh*, no. 34.3.

"These Manifestations of God each have a two-fold station. One is the station of pure abstraction and essential unity. In this respect, if thou callest them all by one name, and dost ascribe to them the same attributes, thou has not erred from the truth . . .

"The other station is the station of distinction, and pertaineth to the world of creation, and to the limitations thereof. In this respect, each Manifestation of God hath a distinct individuality, a definitely prescribed mission, a predestined revelation, and specially designated limitations. Each one of them is known by a different name, is characterized by a special attribute, fulfills a definite mission, and is entrusted with a particular Revelation . . ." Bahá'u'lláh, *Gleanings from the Writings of Bahá'u'lláh*, no. 22.2–4.

What is the relationship between a Messenger and God Himself?

The Messengers of God are like mirrors that reflect the Holy Spirit of God to mankind. They have physical bodies and live a human life, but Their spiritual nature is mysteriously connected directly to God:

"And since there can be no tie of direct intercourse to bind the one true God with His creation, and no resemblance whatever can ex-ist between the transient and the Eternal, the contingent and the Absolute, He hath ordained that in every age and dispensation a pure and stainless Soul be made manifest in the kingdoms of earth and heaven. Unto this subtle, this mysterious and ethereal Being He hath assigned a twofold nature; the physical, pertaining to the world of matter, and the spiritual, which is born of the substance of God Himself. He hath, moreover, conferred upon Him a double station. The first station, which is related to His innermost reality, representeth Him as One Whose voice is the voice of God Himself. To this testifieth the tradition: 'Manifold and mysterious is My relationship with God. I am He, Himself, and He is I, Myself, except that I am that I am, and He is that He is.'" Bahá'u'lláh, *Gleanings from the Writings of Baha'u'llah*, no. 27.4.

How has each revelation been suited to the needs of its time?

"Just as the organic evolution of mankind has been slow and gradual, and involved successively the unification of the family, the tribe, the city-state, and the nation, so has the light vouchsafed by the Revelation of God, at various stages in the evolution of religion, and reflected in the successive Dispensations of the past, been slow and progressive. Indeed the measure of Divine Revelation, in every age, has been adapted to, and commensurate with, the degree of social progress achieved in that age by a constantly evolving humanity." Shoghi Effendi, *The Promised Day is Come,* ¶291.

In what way are the religions of the world like limbs of a tree?

"Religions are like the branches of one Tree. One branch is high, one is low and one in the centre, yet all draw their life from the one stem. One branch bears fruit and others are not laden so abundantly. All the Prophets are lights, they only differ in degree; they shine like brilliant heavenly bodies, each have their appointed place and time of ascension. Some are like lamps, some like the moon, some like distant stars, and a few are like the sun, shining from one end of the earth to the other. All have the same Light to give, yet they are different in degree." 'Abdu'l-Bahá, *'Abdu'l-Bahá in London,* pp. 62–63.

Why have there been disagreements among religions?

Each Messenger of God provides spiritual guidance as well as social laws, such as marriage laws or dietary restrictions. The spiritual principles are the same because they are essential truths, but the social laws vary. When people focus only on the social laws, and insist on following customs initiated by their ancestors instead of examining the spiritual truths, the religions do not seem to agree:

"Each one of the divine religions has established two kinds of ordinances: the essential and the accidental. The essential ordinances rest upon the firm, unchanging, eternal foundations of the Word itself. They concern spiritualities, seek to stabilize morals, awaken intuitive susceptibilities, reveal the knowledge of God and inculcate the love of all mankind. The accidental laws concern the administration of outer human actions and relations, establishing rules and regulations requisite for the world of bodies and their control. These are ever subject to change and supersedure according to exigencies of time, place and condition. . . . [B]y adherence to these temporary laws, blindly following and imitating ancestral forms, difference and divergence have arisen among followers of the various religions, resulting in disunion, strife

and hatred." 'Abdu'l-Bahá, *The Promulgation of Universal Peace*, p. 480.

Do leaders of religion share some of the blame for disunity among the religions?

"Leaders of religion, in every age, have hindered their people from attaining the shores of eternal salvation, inasmuch as they held the reins of authority in their mighty grasp. Some for the lust of leadership, others through want of knowledge and understanding, have been the cause of the deprivation of the people." Bahá'u'lláh, Kitáb-i-Íqán, ¶15.

How have the Messengers of God spoken about each other?

"The holy Manifestations Who have been the Sources or Founders of the various religious systems were united and agreed in purpose and teaching. Abraham, Moses, Zoroaster, Buddha, Jesus, Muḥammad, the Báb and Bahá'u'lláh are one in spirit and reality. Moreover, each Prophet fulfilled the promise of the One Who came before Him and, likewise, Each announced the One Who would follow. Consider how Abraham foretold the coming of Moses, and Moses embodied the Abrahamic statement. Moses prophesied the Messianic cycle, and Christ fulfilled the law of Moses. It is evident, therefore, that the Holy Manifestations Who founded the religious systems are united and agreed; there is no differentiation possible in Their mission and teachings; all are reflectors of reality, and all are promulgators of the religion of God." 'Abdu'l-Bahá, *The Promulgation of Universal Peace,* p. 276.

The Reality of all is One.
Truth is one.

'Abdu'l-Bahá,
'Abdu'l-Bahá in London, p. 62.

The next two pages contain charts demonstrating the close ties among God's Messengers and the religions They founded. Here are some notes pertaining to them:

- **Chart #1 , "The Only Way to God":** Many Messengers of God have declared that there is only one way to reach God—through Themselves—which seems contradictory at first glance. However, as the readings in this chapter have demonstrated, a second look at this spiritual mystery reveals a different explanation. If we think of the Messengers of God as perfect mirrors, we see that each of Them has reflected the Holy Spirit to mankind. Each one has taken a turn being the "only way" for mankind to receive a certain message from God. They were all explaining an essential mystical truth.

- **Chart #2, "The Golden Rule":** This chart contains, in historical order, the "Golden Rule" of seven of the Messengers of God.

The Only Way to God

KRISHNA
Abandoning all duties,
come to Me alone for shelter.
Bhagavad Gita, XVIII–66

MOSES
And Moses alone shall come near the Lord.
Exodus, 24:2

ZOROASTER
There is only one religious way.
This one way is that of good thoughts,
good words, and good deeds.
Gathas, Yasna, 45:5 and 51:2

BUDDHA
This is the path. There is no other that leads
to vision. The way of heaven, of light and of
purity. Of the infinite creator.
Dhammapada, 20:274

JESUS
I am the way, the truth and the life.
No one comes to the Father
except through Me.
John, 14:6

MUḤAMMAD
If anyone seeks guidance elsewhere,
God will lead him astray.
Al-Tirmidhi, Hadith, no. 651

BAHÁ'U'LLÁH
He that hath Me not is bereft of all things.
Turn ye away from all that is on earth
and seek none else but Me.
Bahá'u'lláh, Tablets of Bahá'u'lláh, p. 169

The Golden Rule

KRISHNA
Do naught unto others which would cause you pain if done to you.
Mahabharata, 5:1517

MOSES
[T]hou shalt love thy neighbor as thyself.
Leviticus, 19:18

ZOROASTER
That nature alone is good which refrains from doing unto another whatever is not good for its own self.
Dadistan-i-Dinik, 94:5

BUDDHA
Hurt not others in ways that you yourself would find hurtful.
Udana-varga, 5:18

JESUS
And as ye would that men should do to you, do ye also to them likewise.
Luke, 6:31

MUḤAMMAD
No one of you is a believer until he desires for his brother that which he desires for himself.
Al-Nawawi, Hadith of Al-Nawawi, no. 13

BAHÁ'U'LLÁH
Blessed is he who preferreth his brother before himself.
Bahá'u'lláh, Tablets of Bahá'u'lláh, p. 71

An Outline of Previous Messengers and Their Relationship to the Revelation of Bahá'u'lláh

NOTE: The quotations in the following paragraphs are all from *The Bahá'ís: A Profile of a World Faith and its Worldwide Community.*

KRISHNA, IIINDUISM, DATE UNCERTAIN

"Know thou that when virtue and justice decline in the world, and vice and injustice are enthroned, then I, the Lord, will make myself manifest as a man amongst men and I will destroy evil and injustice." For Bahá'ís who come from a Hindu background, Bahá'u'lláh is the tenth Avatar or the Most Great Spirit destined to come at the end of the Kali Yuga (Dark Age) to establish the Krta Yuga (Golden Age). The purpose of this Most Great Spirit is to rescue mankind from the lowest depths of moral degradation, establish righteousness on the earth and awaken the minds of the people.

MOSES, JUDAISM, C. 1350 BC

For Bahá'ís of Jewish background, Bahá'u'lláh is the appearance of the promised "Lord of Hosts" come down "with ten thousands of saints." A descendent of Abraham and a "scion from the root of Jesse," Bahá'u'lláh has come to provide the way for nations to "beat their swords into plowshares." Bahá'u'lláh's involuntary exile to the Holy Land, along with other historical events, both during His lifetime and afterward, are seen as fulfilling many prophecies in the Old Testament.

ZOROASTER, ZOROASTRIANISM, C. 650 BC

For Bahá'ís of Zoroastrian background, the foretold world savior [Shah Bahram] is Bahá'u'lláh, the Messenger of God Who would appear in Persia to unite all people and renew the world. "When a thousand two hundred and some years have passed from the inception of the religion of the Arabians and the overthrow of the Kingdom and Iran and the degradation of the followers of My religion, a descendent of Iranian Kings will be raised up as a prophet." Bahá'u'lláh was a descendent of the Persian king Yazdegerd the Third and the Bahá'í Faith dates from 1844, which is the year 1260 on the Arabian calendar.

BUDDHA, BUDDHISM, C. 536 BC

For Bahá'ís of Buddhist background, Bahá'u'lláh fulfills the prophecies for the coming of the fifth Buddha, "a Buddha named Maitreye, the Buddha of universal fellowship." This Buddha will bring an age of peace and enlightenment for all humanity. (Christ can be counted as the second Buddha, Muḥammad the third, the Báb as the fourth and Bahá'u'lláh the fifth.)

JESUS, CHRISTIANITY, C. AD 1

For Bahá'ís from a Christian background, Bahá'u'lláh fulfills the promises that Christ made to return "in the Glory of the Father" and as the "Spirit of Truth" Who will lead men unto all truth. His purpose is to bring all people together so that "there shall be one fold, and one shepherd." The declaration of the Báb (the forerunner of Bahá'u'lláh) in 1844 relates to numerous prophecies from the New Testament. In Matthew 24:15, Christ refers to the prophecy of Daniel, which Bible scholars have calculated to work out to exactly 1844. Also, by 1844 Central Africa and China had been opened to Christianity, fulfilling the promise in Matthew 24:14 that ". . . this gospel of the kingdom shall be preached in all the world for a witness unto all nations; and then shall the end come." And the Edict of Toleration that allowed Jews to return to the Holy Land was signed in 1844, fulfilling the prophecy in Luke 21:24 "until the times of the Gentiles be fulfilled . . ."

MUḤAMMAD, ISLAM, AD 622

 For Baháʼís of Muslim background, Baháʼuʼlláh fulfills the promises of the Qurʼán for the "Day of God" and the "Great Announcement," when God will come down "overshadowed with clouds."

Muḥammad described Himself as the "Seal of the Prophets," and in that respect, Baháʼuʼlláh comes not as another prophet in the previous cycle but as the fulfiller of past promises and prophecies Who inaugurates a new cycle.

Man must be a lover of the light, no matter from what dayspring it may appear. He must be a lover of the rose, no matter in what soil it may be growing. He must be a seeker of the truth, no matter from what source it comes. Attachment to the lantern is not loving the light.

ʻAbduʼl-Bahá, *The Promulgation of Universal Peace*, p. 209.

CHAPTER 6

The Greatness of This Day

The Revelation of Bahá'u'lláh

ALL glory be to this Day, the Day in which the fragrances of mercy have been wafted over all created things, a Day so blest that past ages and centuries can never hope to rival it . . .

Bahá'u'lláh, *Tablets of Bahá'u'lláh*, p. 1.

Great indeed is this Day! The allusions made to it in all the sacred Scriptures as the Day of God attest its greatness. The soul of every Prophet of God, of every Divine Messenger, hath thirsted for this wondrous Day. All the divers kindreds of the earth have, likewise, yearned to attain it.

Bahá'u'lláh, *Gleanings from the Writings of Bahá'u'lláh*, no. 7.2.

What is a *Day?*

In Bahá'í terms, *Day* refers to the revelation brought by a specific Messenger of God. In the past, for instance, there was the *Day* of Jesus, the *Day* of Moses, the *Day* of Muḥammad, etc. Right now is the *Day* of Bahá'u'lláh.

How important is this "Day" in human history?

"The purpose underlying all creation is the revelation of this most sublime, this most holy Day, the Day known as the Day of God, in His Books and Scriptures. . . . This is the Day in which God's most excellent favors have been poured out upon men, the Day in which His most mighty grace hath been infused into all created things. . . . A fleeting moment, in this Day, excelleth centuries of a bygone age. . . . The world of being shineth, in this Day, with the resplendency of this Divine Revelation. All created beings extol its saving grace, and sing its praises. The universe is wrapt in an ecstasy of joy and gladness. . . .Well is it with him that hath lived to see this Day and hath recognized its station. . . . This Day a different Sun hath arisen, and a different Heaven hath been adorned with its stars and its planets. The world is another world, and the Cause another Cause. . . . Peerless is this Day, for it is as the eye to past ages and centuries and as a light unto the dark-ness of the times. . . . Should the greatness of this Day be revealed in its fullness, every man would forsake a myriad lives in his longing to partake, though it be for one moment, of its great glory—how much more this world and its corruptible treasures!" Bahá'u'lláh, cited in Shoghi Effendi, *The Advent of Divine Justice,* ¶110.

Is this the beginning of a new spiritual cycle?

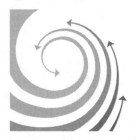

Yes, we are living at the intersection that ends one cycle and begins another. The first cycle, or Prophetic Cycle, is also known as the Adamic Cycle. It stretches back to the beginnings of recorded religious history and contains within it a number of Messengers / Messiahs / Manifestations of God. All of these Messengers prophesied that eventually God would send a Messenger Whose purpose would be to usher in the age of fulfillment, a time when all the previous promises of an era of peace and universal brotherhood would at last come to fruition. Bahá'ís believe that with the dawning of the Bahá'í Era, the cycle of prophecy ended and the cycle of fulfillment, also called the Bahá'í Cycle, began.

How does Bahá'í scripture describe the ending of the Adamic Cycle and the beginning of the Bahá'í Cycle?

"It is evident that every age in which a Manifestation of God hath lived is divinely ordained, and may, in a sense, be characterized as God's appointed Day. This Day, however, is unique, and is to be distinguished from those that have preceded it. The designation "Seal of the Prophets" fully revealeth its high station. The Prophetic Cycle hath, verily, ended. The Eternal Truth is now come. He hath lifted up the Ensign of Power, and is now shedding upon the world the unclouded splendor of His Revelation." Bahá'u'lláh, *Gleanings from the Writings of Bahá'u'lláh*, no. 25.1.

By the righteousness of God! The Mother Book is made manifest, summoning mankind unto God, the Lord of the worlds. . . . The heaven of religions is split and the moon cleft asunder and the peoples of the earth are brought together in a new resurrection.

Bahá'u'lláh, *Tablets of Baha'u'llah*, pp. 247–48.

What is the Bahá'í Cycle and how long will it last?

". . . a universal cycle in the world of existence comprises a vast span of time and countless ages and epochs. In such a cycle, the Manifestations of God shine forth in the visible realm until a universal and supreme Manifestation makes the world the focal centre of divine splendours and, through His revelation, brings it to the stage of maturity. The duration of the cycle He ushers in is very long indeed. Other Manifestations will arise in the course of that cycle under His shadow and will renew, according to the needs of the time, certain laws pertaining to material affairs and transactions, but They will remain under His shadow. We are in the cycle which began with Adam and whose universal Manifestation is Bahá'u'lláh." 'Abdu'l-Bahá, *Some Answered Questions,* no. 41.5.

. . . thou canst imagine the magnitude of the Bahá'í cycle—a cycle that must extend over a period of at least five hundred thousand years.

'Abdu'l-Bahá, cited in Shoghi Effendi, *The World Order of Bahá'u'lláh,* p. 102.

What are some of the special features of the Bahá'í Cycle?

"This is a new cycle of human power. All the horizons of the world are luminous, and the world will become indeed as a garden and a paradise. It is the hour of unity of the sons of men and of the drawing together of all races and all classes. You are loosed from ancient superstitions which have kept men ignorant, destroying the foundation of true humanity.

"The gift of God to this enlightened age is the knowledge of the oneness of mankind and of the fundamental oneness of religion. War shall cease between nations, and by the will of God the Most Great Peace shall come; the world will be seen as a new world, and all men will live as brothers." 'Abdu'l-Bahá, *'Abdu'l-Bahá in London,* p. 19.

What is happening to our world as a result of Bahá'u'lláh's revelation?

"We have, at the bidding of the Omnipotent Ordainer, breathed a new life into every human frame, and instilled into every word a fresh potency. All created things proclaim the evidences of this world-wide regeneration." Bahá'u'lláh, *Gleanings from the Writings of Bahá'u'lláh,* no. 43.2.

"Every single letter proceeding from Our mouth is endowed with such regenerative power as to enable it to bring into existence a new creation— a creation the magnitude of which is inscrutable to all save God." Bahá'u'lláh, cited in Shoghi Effendi, *The Advent of Divine Justice,* ¶111.

"The Call of God, when raised, breathed a new life into the body of mankind, and infused a new spirit into the whole creation. It is for this reason that the world hath been moved to its depths, and the hearts and consciences of men been quickened. Erelong the evidences of this regeneration will be revealed, and the fast asleep will be awakened." 'Abdu'l-Bahá, cited in Shoghi Effendi, *World Order of Bahá'u'lláh,* p. 169.

"As we view the world around us, we are compelled to observe the manifold evidences of that universal fermentation which, in every continent of the globe and in every department of human life, be it religious, social, economic or political, is purging and reshaping humanity in anticipation of the Day when the wholeness of the human race will have been recognized and its unity established." Shoghi Effendi, *The World Order of Bahá'u'lláh,* p. 170.

Does this new revelation signal a change in the maturity of humanity?
"The Revelation of Bahá'u'lláh, whose supreme mission is none other but the achievement of this organic and spiritual unity of the whole body of nations, should . . . be regarded as signalizing through its advent the coming of age of the entire human race. It should be viewed not merely as yet another spiritual revival in the ever-changing fortunes of mankind, not only as a further stage in a chain of progressive Revelations, nor even as the culmination of one of a

series of recurrent prophetic cycles, but rather as marking the last and highest stage in the stupendous evolution of man's collective life on this planet." Shoghi Effendi, *The World Order of Bahá'u'lláh,* p. 163.

Why did the world need a new revelation from God?

"That which was applicable to human needs during the early history of the race can neither meet nor satisfy the demands of this day, this period of newness and consummation . . . The gifts and blessings of the period of youth, although timely and sufficient during the adolescence of mankind, are now incapable of meeting the requirements of its maturity." 'Abdu'l-Bahá, cited in Shoghi Effendi, *The World Order of Bahá'u'lláh,* p. 165.

What do the Bahá'í Writings say about North America?

"The continent of America is, in the eyes of the one true God, the land wherein the splendors of His light shall be revealed, where the mysteries of His Faith shall be unveiled, where the righteous will abide and the free assemble." 'Abdu'l-Bahá, *Tablets of the Divine Plan,* no. 9.3.

"The American continent gives signs and evidences of very great advancement; its future is even more promising, for its influence and illumination are far-reaching, and it will lead all nations spiritually. The flag of freedom and banner of liberty have been unfurled here, but the prosperity and advancement of a city, the happiness and greatness of a country depend upon its hearing and obeying the call of God. The light of reality must shine therein and divine civilization be founded; then the radiance of the Kingdom will be diffused and heavenly influences surround." 'Abdu'l-Bahá, *The Promulgation of Universal Peace,* p. 143.

What special spiritual responsibilities does America have?

"May this American Democracy be the first nation to establish the foundation of international agreement. May it be the first nation to proclaim the unity of mankind. May it be the first to unfurl the Standard of the Most Great Peace." 'Abdu'l-Bahá, *The Promulgation of Universal Peace,* p. 49.

What is the ultimate goal of Bahá'u'lláh's revelation?

"Then will all humankind, because of this fresh and dazzling bounty, be gathered in a single homeland. Then will conflict and dissension vanish from the face of the earth, then will mankind be cradled in love for the beauty of the All-Glorious. Discord will change to accord, dissension to unison. The roots of malevolence will be torn out, the basis of aggression destroyed. The bright rays of union will obliterate the darkness of limitations, and the splendors of heaven will make the human heart to be even as a mine veined richly with the love of God." 'Abdu'l-Bahá, *Selections from the Writings of 'Abdu'l-Bahá,* no. 7.1.

Is peace really possible?

"The Sun of Truth hath risen above the horizon of this world and cast down its beams of guidance. Eternal grace is never interrupted, and a fruit of that everlasting grace is universal peace. Rest thou assured that in this era of the spirit, the Kingdom of Peace will raise up its tabernacle on the summits of the world, and the commandments of the Prince of Peace will so dominate the arteries and nerves of every people as to draw into His sheltering shade all the nations on earth. From springs of love and truth and unity will the true Shepherd give His sheep to drink." 'Abdu'l-Bahá, *Selections from the Writings of 'Abdu'l-Bahá,* no. 201.1.

What lies beyond the establishment of peace among the nations?

"Permanent peace among nations is an essential stage, but not, Bahá'u'lláh asserts, the ultimate goal of the social development of humanity. Beyond the initial armistice forced upon the world by the fear of nuclear holocaust, beyond the political peace reluctantly entered into by suspicious rival nations, beyond pragmatic arrangements for security and coexistence, beyond even the many experiments in cooperation which these steps will make possible lies the crowning goal: the unification of all the peoples of the world in one universal family." Universal House of Justice, *Messages from the Universal House of Justice 1963–1986,* no. 483.53.

A Prayer for Peace:

"O Thou kind Lord! Thou hast created all humanity from the same stock. Thou hast decreed that all shall belong to the same household. In Thy Holy Presence they are all Thy servants, and all mankind are sheltered beneath Thy Tabernacle; all have gathered together at Thy Table of Bounty; all are illumined through the light of Thy Providence.

O God! Thou art kind to all, Thou hast provided for all, dost shelter all, conferrest life upon all. Thou hast endowed each and all with talents and faculties, and all are submerged in the Ocean of Thy Mercy.

O Thou kind Lord! Unite all. Let the religions agree and make the nations one, so that they may see each other as one family and the whole earth as one home. May they all live together in perfect harmony.

O God! Raise aloft the banner of the oneness of mankind.

O God! Establish the Most Great Peace.

Cement Thou, O God, the hearts together.

O Thou kind Father, God! Gladden our hearts through the fragrance of Thy love. Brighten our eyes through the Light of Thy Guidance. Delight our ears with the melody of Thy Word, and shelter us all in the Stronghold of Thy Providence.

Thou art the Mighty and Powerful, Thou art the Forgiving and Thou art the One Who overlooketh the shortcomings of all mankind." 'Abdu'l-Bahá, *The Promulgation of Universal Peace,* p. 138.

CHAPTER 7

A Little Religious History

During the early 1800s, followers of several different religions came to believe that important prophecies in their sacred writings would soon be fulfilled.

In Europe, several Christian groups found what they considered to be clear Biblical evidence supporting the impending return of Christ. A band of German Templars actually moved to the foot of Mt. Carmel in Israel to await His advent, and the houses they built there still stand.

In America, the Millerites came to much the same conclusion, focusing on the dates of 1843 and 1844. In Central and South America there were ancient Indian prophecies with similar indications, such as Quetzalcoatl's promise to return in the thirteenth Toltec / Aztec era, which would correspond to sometime during the 1800s.

In the Middle East, the focus was on the Koran and Islamic traditions, which indicated the impending arrival of the Qa'im (the Mahdi, the return of the twelfth Imam of Muḥammad) as well as the Day of Resurrection.

Bahá'ís believe that all of these expectations were fulfilled by the appearance of two Messengers from God—the Báb and Bahá'u'lláh—Who appeared during the 1800s with complementary revelations. Bahá'u'lláh was preceded by the Báb, Who was a Messenger of God in His own right, yet also served in a manner analogous to that of Elijah and John the Baptist.

The Báb was martyred in 1850. Bahá'u'lláh died in 1892 and, in His will, appointed His son 'Abdu'l-Bahá to guide the Bahá'í Faith.

'Abdu'l-Bahá died in 1921 and in His will, appointed His grandson Shoghi Effendi as the Guardian of the Bahá'í Faith. After the death of Shoghi Effendi in 1957, there were enough Bahá'ís in the world to elect and sustain the Universal House of Justice. The Universal House of Justice is the administrative body anticipated by Bahá'u'lláh as the international authority for the Bahá'í Faith.

CHAPTER 8

The Báb (the Gate)

1819–1850

The history of the Bahá'í Faith begins with the gentle man Who became known as the Báb. He was meek in manner yet decisively firm in the declaration of His mission. His life was short and ended tragically with His martyrdom when He was just thirty years old.

When and where was the Báb born?

The Báb was born on October 20, 1819, in Shiraz, Iran. His parents were Siyyid Muḥammad-Riḍá, a merchant in Shiraz, and his wife, Fátimih Bagum. Both of them were descendants of Muḥammad. They named their new baby 'Ali-Muḥammad.

If His birthname was 'Alí-Muḥammad, why is He called the Báb?

When 'Alí-Muḥammad announced His mission as a Messenger of God in 1844, He took the title of *Báb*, which means *gate*. This description of Himself as a gate emphasized that one of His spiritual functions was to open people's hearts and make them ready to accept a second Messenger of God who would soon appear. Bahá'ís believe that this second Messenger was Bahá'u'lláh.

What was the early life of the Báb like?

The Báb's father died soon after the Báb was born, and a maternal uncle took responsibility for the Báb and His mother. At the age of six or seven, the Báb was sent to school. As a young teenager, He left school and joined His uncle's business, where He worked for several years. In 1842, when He was twenty, the Báb married Khadíjih Bagum. They had one son, who died shortly after birth.

What were the two spiritual stations of the Báb?

The Báb was a Messenger of God Who founded a new religion, the Bábí Faith, but He was also the Herald of Bahá'u'lláh.

First, the Báb announced that He was a Messenger of God and the Promised One of Islám—the Qá'im or Mahdi.

". . . I am the One whose name you have for a thousand years invoked, at whose mention you have risen, whose advent you have longed to witness, and the hour of whose Revelation you have prayed God to hasten. Verily I say, it is incumbent upon the peoples of both the East and the West to obey My word and to pledge allegiance to My person." The Báb, cited in Nabíl-i-A'zam, *The Dawn-Breakers,* pp. 315–16.

Second, the Báb explained that He was the Forerunner or Herald of a second Messenger, One far greater than Himself Who would ful-fill the redemption of humanity Whom He described as "Him Whom God shall make manifest." The Báb repeatedly advised His followers to watch for the imminent advent of this Messenger, and Bahá'ís accept Bahá'u'lláh as that Messenger.

When and where did the Báb announce His mission as a Messenger of God?

On May 23, 1844, a few hours after sunset, in the town of Shiraz, Iran, the Báb announced His mission to Mullá Ḥusayn, an earnest young man who had spent many years studying the signs and dates in the Koran and other holy books concerning the coming of the next Messenger of God.

How did Mullá Ḥusayn describe the experience of hearing the Báb announce Himself as a Messenger of God?

He described it as a thunderbolt that struck with such force that he felt temporarily paralyzed:

"I was blinded by its dazzling splendor and overwhelmed by its crushing force. Excitement, joy, awe, and wonder stirred the depths of my soul." Mullá Ḥusayn, cited in Shoghi Effendi, *God Passes By,* p. 8.

In what majestic terms did the Báb describe His relationship to God?

I am the Primal Point from which have been generated all created things . . . I am the Countenance of God Whose splendor can never be obscured, the light of God whose radiance can never fade . . . All the keys of heaven God hath chosen to place on My right hand, and all the keys of hell on My left . . . I am one of the sustaining pillars of the primal Word of God. Whosoever hath recognized Me, hath known all that is true and right, and hath attained all that is good and seemly . . .

The Báb, cited in Shoghi Effendi, *The World Order of Bahá'u'lláh,* p. 126.

What else did the Báb say to Mullá Ḥusayn?

"This night, this very hour will, in the days to come, be celebrated as one of the greatest and most significant of all festivals. Render thanks to God for having graciously assisted you to attain your heart's desire. . . . Eighteen souls must, in the beginning, spontaneously and of their own accord, accept Me and recognize the truth of My Revelation. Unwarned and uninvited, each of these must seek independently to find Me." The Báb, cited in Nabíl-i-A'ẓam, *The Dawn-Breakers,* pp. 61–63.

Did seventeen more people independently find the Báb?

During the three months following the Báb's declaration to Mullá Ḥusayn, seventeen other people, including one woman, discovered and recognized the Báb through their own spiritual investigations. These first eighteen believers were given the title of "Letters of the Living" and were sent by the Báb to spread His message throughout the region.

Who was the woman who independently discovered and recognized the Báb and became a "Letter of the Living?"

Her birthname was Fáṭimih Zarrín-Táj and she was already a renowned poetess when she became a follower of the Báb. The Báb bestowed the name Ṭáhirih on her, which means "the pure one," and she was an outspoken teacher of the Bábí Faith as well as a staunch champion of women's rights. Her husband divorced her because of these activities, and ultimately she was arrested, found guilty of heresy, and put to death by strangulation.

What happened to those who accepted the Báb?

An astonishingly large number of people accepted the message of the Báb, which alarmed the clergy as well as the government, and they immediately tried to destroy the new faith. Many of the Báb's followers were tortured and thousands were killed between 1844 and 1854. One of the earliest western accounts of these atrocities was featured in *The London Times* in 1845. Under the title "Mahometan Schism," it reported the arrest of four of the Báb's earliest followers, who were punished for abandoning Islam by having their beards set on fire and then being led through the city by strings through their noses.

What happened to the Báb Himself?

The Báb was imprisoned in 1847, less than three years after He announced His mission. During His imprisonment, He was bastinadoed (twenty lashes were administered to the bottoms of His feet). In 1850 He was brought to trial for blasphemy and apostasy. Eventually, He was sentenced to death.

When did the Báb die?

The Báb was executed by a firing squad on July 9, 1850, in the city of Tabriz, Iran. He was only thirty years old.

Where was the Báb buried?

After the martyrdom of the Báb, some of His followers managed to gather the remains of His body, place them in a casket, and hide it in a safe place. In AD 1899, the casket was laboriously moved from Iran to Palestine (present-day Israel) by Bahá'ís who carried it overland to Beirut and then by sea to 'Akká.

A few years later, 'Abdu'l-Bahá entombed the remains of the Báb in a stone mausoleum built on the side of Mt. Carmel in Haifa. Following that, a shrine was erected atop the mausoleum. In 2008, the Shrine of the Báb was designated as a World Heritage Site.

A Prayer of the Báb

Say: God sufficeth all things above all things, and nothing in the heavens or in the earth but God sufficeth. Verily, He is in Himself the Knower, the Sustainer, the Omnipotent.

The Báb, *Selections from the Writings of the Báb*, no. 4:8:2.

CHAPTER 9

Bahá'u'lláh (the Glory of God)

1817–1892

The second part of the history of the Bahá'í Faith centers around Bahá'u'lláh. Acknowledged in His youth as wise beyond His years, He became a Bábí while in His twenties and was imprisoned and then exiled for His beliefs. In 1863, He announced that He was the Messenger of God foretold by the Báb, which led to further banishment and imprisonment until His death in 1892.

Where and when was Bahá'u'lláh born?

In 1817, in Tehran, Persia (now Iran), a son was born to a noble family from the province of Nur. He was a descendant of Abraham as well as a descendant of David on His mother's side.

The name His parents gave Him was Mírzá Ḥusayn-'Alí. He adopted the title of *Bahá* when He was still a follower of the Báb, and was eventually known by the longer title *Bahá'u'lláh*.

What was Bahá'u'lláh like when He was young?

Although He had virtually no formal education, even as a child He was renowned for the breadth of His knowledge and for His extraordinary insights into difficult passages of the Qur'án.

As Bahá'u'lláh grew older, He was known as the defender of the oppressed and gave freely of His wealth to the poor. When His father died, the Persian government offered Him the same position, but He refused. The Prime Minister was not surprised, saying "Such a position is unworthy of Him. . . I cannot understand Him, but I am convinced that He is destined for some lofty career. His thoughts are not like ours." *The Dawn-Breakers,* p. 106.

When did Bahá'u'lláh become a follower of the Báb?

Bahá'u'lláh accepted the message of the Báb in 1844, soon after the Báb's declaration. He then arose to promulgate its teachings and share the sufferings of its followers. At one point He was bastinadoed (the soles of His feet were beaten with a stick) and imprisoned.

What happened after Bahá'u'lláh became a Bábí?

In 1852, Bahá'u'lláh's possessions were confiscated and He was arrested. He, along with a number of fellow followers of the Báb, were then confined for four months in a dark and filthy underground dungeon referred to as "the Black Pit." The weight of the heavy iron collar and chains used to bind Him injured His neck and left marks that remained for the rest of His life. Bahá'u'lláh later wrote: "We were all huddled together in one cell, our feet in stocks, and around our necks fastened the most galling

of chains. The air we breathed was laden with the foulest impurities, while the floor on which we sat was covered with filth and infested with vermin. No ray of light was allowed to penetrate that pestilential dungeon or to warm its icy-coldness. We were placed in two rows, each facing the other." Bahá'u'lláh, cited in Nabil-i-A'ẓam, *The Dawn-Breakers,* p. 631.

How did Bahá'u'lláh encourage the other prisoners to withstand the rigors of their agonizing imprisonment?

"We had taught them to repeat certain verses which, every night they chanted with extreme fervour. 'God is sufficient unto me; He verily is the All-sufficing!' one row would intone, while the other would reply: 'In Him let the trusting trust. . .'"

"Every day Our gaolers [jailers], entering Our cell, would call the name of one of Our companions, bidding him arise and follow them to the foot of the gallows. With what eagerness would the owner of that name respond to that solemn call! Relieved of his chains, he would spring to his feet and, in a state of uncontrollable delight, would approach and embrace Us. We would seek to comfort him with the assurance of an everlasting life in the world beyond, and,

filling his heart with hope and joy, would send him forth to win the crown of glory. He would embrace, in turn, the rest of his fellow-prisoners and then proceed to die as dauntlessly as he had lived." Bahá'u'lláh, cited in Nabíl-i-A'ẓam, *The Dawn-Breakers,* pp. 632–33.

What spiritual experience did Bahá'u'lláh have while in prison?

"During the days I lay in the prison of Ṭihrán, though the galling weight of the chains and the stench-filled air allowed Me but little sleep, still in those infrequent moments of slumber I felt as if something flowed from the crown of My head over My breast, even as a mighty torrent that precipitateth itself upon the earth from the summit of a lofty mountain. Every limb of My body would, as a result, be set afire. At such moments My tongue recited what no man could bear to hear." Bahá'u'lláh, Epistle to the Son of the Wolf, p. 22.

How did Bahá'u'lláh realize He was the Messenger of God promised by the Báb?

"While engulfed in tribulations I heard a most wondrous, a most sweet voice, calling above My head. Turning My face, I beheld a Maiden—the embodiment of the remembrance of the name of My Lord—suspended in the air before Me. . . . Betwixt earth and heaven she was raising a call which captivated the hearts and minds of men." Bahá'u'lláh, *The Summons of the Lord of Hosts,* ¶6.

"I was but a man like others, asleep upon My couch, when lo, the breezes of the All-Glorious were wafted over Me, and taught Me the knowledge of all that hath been. This thing is not from Me, but from One Who is Almighty and All-Knowing. And He bade Me lift up My voice between earth and heaven, and for this there befell Me what hath caused the tears of every man of understanding to flow." Bahá'u'lláh, Epistle to the Son of the Wolf, p. 11.

How did Bahá'u'lláh describe His revelation?

"The Divine Springtime is come, O Most Exalted Pen, for the Festival of the All-Merciful is fast approaching. . . . Take heed lest anything deter thee from extolling the greatness of this Day—the Day whereon the Finger of majesty and power hath opened the seal of the Wine of Reunion, and called all who are in the heavens and all who are on the earth. . . . the Day whereon He Who is the Desire of all nations hath shed upon the kingdoms of the unseen and of the seen the splendor of the light of His most excellent names, and enveloped them with the radiance of the luminaries of His most gracious favors—favors which none can reckon except Him, Who is the omnipotent Protector of the entire creation." Bahá'u'lláh, *Gleanings from the Writings of Bahá'u'lláh,* nos. 14.1, 14.2, 14.14.

What happened after Bahá'u'lláh was released from prison?

Bahá'u'lláh was released from prison in December, 1852 and banished from Persia. Declining the protection of the Russian government offered by its minister, Prince Dolgorukov, He proceeded to Baghdad. His wife and two of His children accompanied Him, but the youngest child had to be left behind with friends because it would be impossible for him to endure the long winter trek through snow-covered mountains.

Bahá'u'lláh and His family remained in exile in Baghdad until 1863 and then were banished again, this time to Constantinople (now Istanbul, Turkey). Before leaving Baghdad, He stayed for twelve days in a tent pitched on a small but beautifully landscaped island just outside the city, a spot now known as the Garden of Riḍván or *Garden of Paradise.* During this time, He announced that the prophecies of the Báb had been fulfilled and that He, Bahá'u'lláh, was the promised Manifestation of God. His title, *Bahá'u'lláh,* means *Glory of God.*

How long did Bahá'u'lláh live in Turkey?

Within a few months of arriving in Constantinople, Bahá'u'lláh was sent further north, to Adrianople (now Edirne, Turkey). In Adrianople there was a very favorable public response to His teachings, which aroused the animosity of the clergy, and in 1868, He was banished to the remote Turkish penal colony of 'Akká.

How long was Bahá'u'lláh imprisoned in 'Akká?

Bahá'u'lláh spent more than two years inside the grim prison citadel before He was allowed to live in a modest house that lay within the walls of the small city. The charges against

Him were never officially withdrawn, but after nine years of confinement in 'Akká. He was given permission to move into the countryside. Eventually He and His family settled in a house known as *Bahjí* (Delight), where He lived for the rest of His life. From time to time He would travel around to the other side of the bay and camp on the slope of Mount Carmel. His son, 'Abdu'l-Bahá, later pointed out that when Bahá'u'lláh was camping, His tent was on the very spot where, according to ancient prophecies, the Glory of God would be manifested in the latter days.

SIMPLIFIED MAP OF THE EXILES OF BAHÁ'U'LLÁH

This map uses current boundaries and names

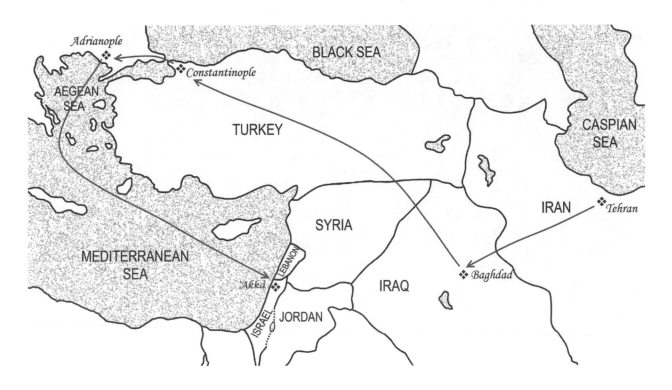

How did Bahá'u'lláh spend the last years of His life?

During the last years of His life, Bahá'u'lláh devoted most of His time to writing and to receiving a constant stream of visitors and pilgrims who wanted to learn more about His teachings. Many of those who became His followers moved to other countries in order to introduce the Bahá'í Faith to new groups of people.

Edward G. Browne, a physician and professor of Arabic at the University of Cambridge was the only Westerner to actually meet Bahá'u'lláh. Of this experience he wrote: "The face of him on whom I gazed I can never forget, though I cannot describe it. Those piercing eyes seemed to read one's very soul; power and authority sat on that ample brow. . . . No need to ask in whose presence I stood, as I bowed myself before one who is the object of a devotion and love which kings might envy and emperors sigh for in vain!" Edward G Browne, cited in Shoghi Effendi, *God Passes By,* p. 194.

Where is Bahá'u'lláh buried?

After Bahá'u'lláh's passing on May 29, 1892, His body was laid to rest in a small stone house adjacent to Bahjí, the house where He had been living. The gardens surrounding Bahjí have been beautifully enlarged, and the house has been restored and filled with photos and relics. Thousands of pilgrims from around the world visit the site each year.

CHAPTER 10

'Abdu'l-Bahá

1844–1921

The third phase of the Bahá'í Faith is centered on 'Abdu'l-Bahá, the son of Bahá'u'lláh. Although not a Messenger of God, He has a unique station as the Center of Bahá'u'lláh's Covenant. As a child, He accompanied His Father into exile, and for most of His life He remained a prisoner of the Ottoman Empire, forced to live in Palestine. He was cherished for His kindness and generosity, and He was the constant educator and encourager of the early communities of Bahá'ís, including those in the Western world.

When and where was 'Abdu'l-Bahá born?

'Abdu'l-Bahá was born in Tehran on the same day that the Báb declared Himself as a Manifestation of God—May 23, 1844. His parents were Bahá'u'lláh and Ásíyih Khánum, also known as Navváb. They named their new son 'Abbás and often called Him 'Abbás Effendi (*Effendi* means *sir*).

'Abdu'l-Bahá's birth, the same day as the Báb's declaration, was a symbol of the significance of His life as a central figure in the Bahá'í Faith. It also presaged the sacrifices He would be called upon to make, and the services He would render to His Father and to Bahá'ís around the world.

What was His early childhood like?

For the first six years, 'Abdu'l-Bahá enjoyed a happy and carefree life. His family was wealthy and possessed beautiful houses in both the city and the country. As was customary for children of the nobility, He received little formal education.

What happened during the rest of 'Abdu'l-Bahá's childhood?

At the age of seven, He became so ill with tuberculosis that He was expected to die. The illness eventually faded, but He was troubled by recurring coughs and lung problems for the rest of His life.

When He was just eight years old, His Father was arrested and imprisoned. Shortly thereafter, the family's home was looted, which immediately plunged His mother and two siblings into poverty. Neighborhood children began to taunt and threaten 'Abdu'l-Bahá whenever He left the house. His mother was able to rescue a few things, such as the jeweled buttons from her wedding clothes, and she sold them to buy food and other necessities. When this money ran out, she was forced to borrow from relatives.

Did 'Abdu'l-Bahá visit Bahá'u'lláh in prison?

'Abdu'l-Bahá insisted on visiting Bahá'u'lláh in the Black Pit, and He was heartbroken at seeing the injuries caused by the iron collar and chains around His Father's neck. "I saw a dark, steep place," He later remembered. "We entered a small, narrow doorway, and went down two steps, but beyond those one could see nothing. In the middle of the stairway, all of a sudden we heard [Bahá'u'lláh's]. . . voice: 'Do not bring him in here,' and so they took me back." 'Abdu'l-Bahá, cited in Balyuzi, *'Abdu'l-Bahá: The Centre of the Covenant of Bahá'u'lláh,* p. 11.

What happened when Bahá'u'lláh was released?

When His Father was released from prison and banished from His homeland, 'Abdu'l-Bahá accompanied His parents on the grim wintertime trek through the mountains to Baghdad. It was so cold that 'Abdu'l-Bahá suffered from frostbite during the journey.

What did 'Abdu'l-Bahá do as He got a little older?

Both of 'Abdu'l-Bahá's parents spent a great deal of time teaching Him to read fluently and write with clarity. He also practiced writing by handcopying the writings of the Báb. By the time He was twelve, He was managing many of the household's affairs. Soon after that, He began to serve as His Father's secretary and also interviewed people who wished to come and speak with Bahá'u'lláh.

What was life like in the prison of 'Akká?

'Abdu'l-Bahá was twenty-four years old when the final exile forced Bahá'u'lláh and the family into the prison at 'Akká. Because the prison was filthy and the food unfit to eat, almost everyone succumbed to dysentery, typhoid fever, or malaria. 'Abdu'l-Bahá nursed those who were ill until He, too, was overtaken by dysentery. After recovering, He gradually made friends among the prison guards and then, when He was allowed to go outside the prison walls, 'Abdu'l-Bahá became familiar with many of the townspeople. When the restictions on the family were relaxed, 'Abdu'l-Bahá was the one Who was able to find a place for all of them to live.

Did 'Abdu'l-Bahá ever marry?

In 1873, He married Fáṭimih Nahri, also known as Munírih (*Luminous*). They had nine children, but only four of them, all girls, survived to adulthood.

How did Bahá'u'lláh show His own great respect for His son?

'Abdu'l-Bahá was given several meaningful titles by Bahá'u'lláh, including the *Most Great Branch, the Mystery of God,* and *the Master.* Before Bahá'u'lláh died in 1892, He wrote a will appointing 'Abdu'l-Bahá as the authorized interpreter of His writings:

"'When the ocean of My presence hath ebbed and the Book of My Revelation is ended, turn your faces toward Him Whom God hath purposed, Who hath branched from this Ancient Root.' The object of this sacred verse is none other except the Most Mighty Branch ['Abdu'l-Bahá]." Bahá'u'lláh, *Tablets of Bahá'u'lláh,* p. 221.

When did 'Abbás begin using the title of 'Abdu'l-Bahá?

It was only after His Father's ascension that 'Abbás Effendi chose the title of 'Abdu'l-Bahá, generally translated as *Servant of Bahá.* With this name, He wanted to show clearly that His relationship to Bahá'u'lláh and to the Bahá'í Faith was one of utter servitude. He was not a Manifestation of God but is understood as a Mystery of God. He served as the authoritative interpreter of Bahá'u'lláh's writings and guided the growth of the Bahá'í Faith until His passing in 1921.

How did Shoghi Effendi describe the qualities and station of 'Abdu'l-Bahá?

"He gets His light, His inspiration and sustenance direct from the Fountainhead of the Bahá'í Revelation; He reflects even as a clear and perfect Mirror the rays of Bahá'u'lláh's glory and does not inherently possess that indefinable yet all-pervading reality the exclusive possession of which is the hallmark of Prophethood; His words are not equal in rank, though they possess an equal validity with the utterances of Bahá'u'lláh." Shoghi Effendi, *World Order of Bahá'u'lláh,* p. 139.

Was 'Abdu'l-Bahá ever able to leave Palestine?

When the Sultan of the Ottoman Empire was removed by the Young Turks' revolution in 1908, 'Abdu'l-Bahá was set free from what had been forty years of confinement in the Holy Land. And so, in 1911, Abdu'l-Bahá journeyed to both Europe and North America to proclaim Bahá'u'lláh's message and provide encouragement to the early groups of Bahá'ís. He returned to Palestine shortly before the outbreak of World War I.

Why was 'Abdu'l-Bahá knighted?

During the First World War, Palestine suffered severe food shortages and, 'Abdu'l-Bahá devoted great time and effort to supplying aid to those in distress, including the distribution of grain from His own stockpile. In 1920, He was knighted for this service by the British government.

How did 'Abdu'l-Bahá nurture the growth of the Bahá'í Faith?

At the time of Bahá'u'lláh's passing, there were approximately 50,000 Bahá'ís in the world. The Faith had spread to most countries and territories in the Middle East and to the Indian subcontinent, but Bahá'u'lláh and His teachings were as yet unknown in Europe, the Americas, sub-Saharan Africa, Australasia, and most of Asia. 'Abdu'l-Bahá welcomed numerous visits by pilgrims and spent time educating them about the Bahá'í Faith. With His encouragement, many of them were able to begin teaching others about the new religion and the number of believers in the world doubled. He also wrote several books plus numerous letters that elucidated Bahá'u'lláh's teachings and delineated the distinctive features of the Administrative Order of the Bahá'í Faith.

When did 'Abdu'l-Bahá die?

He passed away at the age of seventy-seven on November 28, 1921. Because 'Abdu'l-Bahá had befriended so many people throughout Palestine,

His death produced an unprecedented outpouring of emotion and admiration. Jews, Christians, Muslims, Druzes, and Bahá'ís, as well as Arabs, Turks, Kurds, Armenians, and other ethnic groups, were united in their common grief.

The funeral drew ten thousand people, including the British High Commissioner and the Governor of Jerusalem. The coffin, followed by a long train of mourners, was carried up the slope of Mount Carmel to the Shrine of the Báb. Nine speakers, representing several faiths, delivered orations. Afterward, the coffin was placed in a vault adjoining the one containing the remains of the Báb.

CHAPTER 11

Shoghi Effendi

1897–1957

In 1921, Shoghi Effendi became the Guardian of the Bahá'í Faith because He was appointed to that position in the will of 'Abdu'l-Bahá. 'Abdu'l-Bahá described Shoghi Effendi as "the sign of God, the chosen branch, the guardian of the Cause of God . . . the expounder of the words of God" ('Abdu'l-Bahá, *Will and Testament of 'Abdu'l-Bahá,* p. 11).

At that point there were only about 100,000 Bahá'ís in the world, most of them living in the Middle East. Shoghi Effendi dedicated the rest of his life to directing the growth of the Bahá'í Faith and helping its believers withstand the many challenges of being members of a new religion.

Who were Shoghi Effendi's parents?

Shoghi Effendi was born March 1, 1897 in 'Akká to Díyá'íyyih Khánum (the eldest daughter of 'Abdu'l-Bahá) and Mírzá Hádí Shírází (one of the maternal relatives of the Báb).

What was his childhood like?

Shoghi Effendi spent much of his early childhood near his grandfather, 'Abdu'l-Bahá, who taught him to memorize and chant prayers. Along with the other Bahá'ís living in Palestine at that time, he learned to bear verbal abuse and was sometimes threatened with physical attacks.

How did Shoghi Effendi come by his name?

His birth name was simply Shoghi, and he might ultimately have been called by the last name of *Shírází*, like his father, but 'Abdu'l-Bahá gave him the last name *Rabbani* to distinguish him from his cousins. 'Abdu'l-Bahá also insisted, even when Shoghi was a child, that *Effendi*, meaning *sir* or *mister*, be used with his name at all times.

Where was Shoghi Effendi educated?

After studying with his cousins at home for a few years, he was sent to a French Christian Brothers school in Haifa. After that he went to a boarding school in Beirut and then attended the American University in Beirut. His final degree was from Balliol College, Oxford. Because 'Abdu'l-Bahá stressed the importance of being multilingual, Shoghi Effendi became fluent in Persian, Turkish, Arabic, French, and English. The wide scope of his education gave him views into both Eastern and Western culture, something that proved invaluable to his future work as the translator of many of the Bahá'í writings and the Guardian of the young but already international religion of his great-grandfather.

Did Shoghi Effendi ever marry and have children?

In 1937, he married a Canadian woman, Mary Maxwell, also known as Rúḥíyyih Khánum. They did not have any children.

How was Shoghi Effendi appointed as Guardian?

When Shoghi Effendi was twenty-four, still studying in England, 'Abdu'l-Bahá died. In his will, 'Abdu'l-Bahá appointed Shoghi Effendi Rabbani as Guardian of the Bahá'í Faith. The institution of the Guardianship had been anticipated in portions of Bahá'u'lláh's writings, and this appointment made it reality.

Was Shoghi Effendi surprised by being appointed Guardian?

Shoghi Effendi was heartbroken by the death of his grandfather, but he immediately obeyed

'Abdul-l-Bahá's wishes and left England for the Holy Land, where he began the task of guiding the Bahá'ís of the world.

Then, in April of 1922, overwhelmed by the mental and physical strain of his new position, he took a leave of absence in order to gather himself, recover his health, and figure out how to come to terms with what would be the life-long burden of being the Guardian. Mr. Leroy Ioas recalled some of what he heard from Shoghi Effendi in the following remembrance:

Shoghi Effendi was a very remarkable young man, and of course he just worshiped 'Abdu'l-Bahá. And when 'Abdu'l-Bahá passed away, the whole world became dark for him. All light had gone out. When he returned to the Holy Land, he had in mind, from the things which 'Abdu'l-Bahá had said to him that "'Abdu'l-Bahá would give me the honor of . . . calling together the great conclave which would elect the Universal House of Justice. And I thought in His Will and Testament that that was probably what He was instructing be done."

"But," he said, "instead of that I found that I was appointed the Guardian of the Cause of God. . . . I didn't want to be the Guardian of the Cause. [In the] first place, I didn't think that I was worthy. Next place, I didn't want to face these responsibilities. . . . I didn't want to be the Guardian. I knew what it meant. I knew that my life as a human being was over. . . . I didn't want it and I didn't want to face it.

So . . . I left the Holy Land, and I went up into the mountains of Switzerland, and I fought with myself until I conquered myself. Then I came back and I turned myself over to God and I was the Guardian." Talk by Leroy Ioas, cited in *Youth Can Move the World,* p. 33.

How did Shoghi Effendi guide the growth of the Bahá'í Faith?

Shoghi Effendi guided the development of the Bahá'í Faith through an outpouring of letters and plans. He explained the implications of Bahá'u'lláh's teachings on issues ranging from family life to Bahá'í administration and world government. He also elaborated on the relationship of the Bahá'í Faith to other religions and doctrines and encouraged widespread teaching and service around the world. Because of his ceaseless efforts, Bahá'u'lláh's message soon spread to every corner of the globe.

When Shoghi Effendi was appointed Guardian, there were approximately 100,000 Bahá'ís. Most were Iranian or Middle Eastern with a handful in India, Europe, and North America and others widely scattered in a total of thirty-five countries. During Shoghi Effendi's ministry there was a fourfold increase in the number of Bahá'ís. The number of countries, territories, and colonies in which they lived rose to more than 250.

In 1953, Shoghi Effendi launched the most ambitious undertaking in the history of this young religion—a global plan which he termed the "Ten Year World Crusade." This plan was set to conclude in 1963, the centenary of the declaration of Bahá'u'lláh in the Garden of Riḍván. By that date, 132 new countries and major territories were to be opened to the Bahá'í Faith and National Spiritual Assemblies were to be established in most countries in Europe and Latin America.

When did Shoghi Effendi die?

In early November, 1957, while he was visiting England to purchase furnishings for the Bahá'í archives building on Mount Carmel, Shoghi Effendi contracted flu and became severely ill. On November 4, he died of a heart attack, leaving the Bahá'í world stunned and its ten-year plan only half completed. Because he died childless and without appointing a successor, there could be no second Guardian.

Where is he buried?

In accord with Bahá'í law, Shoghi Effendi was buried less than an hour's travel from his place of death, in New Southgate Cemetery in London. A tall Corinthian column surmounted by an eagle marks his grave.

How did the Bahá'ís of the world cope with the death of Shoghi Effendi?

At first, the Bahá'ís were unsure what should happen next. However, in one of his last messages to the Bahá'í world, Shoghi Effendi named the Hands of the Cause (chapter 13) as the "Chief Stewards" of the Bahá'í Faith. Their assignment was to collaborate closely with the National Spiritual Assemblies to carry out the ten-year plan and protect the unity of the Bahá'í Faith.

With this message in hand, the Hands of the Cause went forward with the ten-year plan. And, after studying the writings of Bahá'u'lláh and 'Abdu'l-Bahá, decided that the first Universal House of Justice should be elected in 1963. The election would be an event of overwhelming importance because this new institution had been envisioned by Bahá'u'lláh Himself, would be patterned on principles laid down in the writings of both Bahá'u'lláh and 'Abdu'l-Bahá, and would continue to be guided by the institution of the Guardianship through Shoghi Effendi's voluminous writings.

CHAPTER 12

The Covenant and the Universal House of Justice

"And the bow shall be in the cloud; and I will look upon it, that I may remember the everlasting covenant between God and every living creature of all flesh that is upon the earth." Genesis 9:16.

What is a covenant?

In religion, a covenant is an agreement between God and man. God guarantees certain blessings or gives special bounties to mankind, but in return, He expects people to adhere to certain moral standards and behave in accord with the teachings given by His divine Messengers.

What are the types of religious covenants?

There are two different types of covenant that have operated in religions over the course of human history. The first is referred to as a **Greater Covenant** and the second as a **Lesser Covenant**.

What does a Greater Covenant cover?

In this type of covenant, a Messenger of God promises that in due time God will bless mankind with another Messenger. The promise is typically made in the form of prophetic warnings and may contain reminders about the importance of recognizing the new Messenger when He appears.

What are some examples of a Greater Covenant?

"The holy Manifestations Who have been the Sources or Founders of the various religious systems were united and agreed in purpose and teaching. . . . Moreover, each Prophet fulfilled the promise of the One Who came before Him and, likewise, Each announced the One Who would follow. Consider how Abraham foretold the coming of Moses, and Moses embodied the Abrahamic statement. Moses prophesied the Messianic cycle, and Christ fulfilled the law of Moses." 'Abdu'l-Bahá, *The Promulgation of Universal Peace*, p. 276.

What is a Lesser Covenant?

A Lesser Covenant indicates the person to whom the followers should turn for guidance when the current Messenger has died. Christ referred to the importance of Peter, and Muḥammad indicated that 'Alí should be His successor, but these were verbal statements. Perhaps this was because something more concrete would not have been appropriate at that time in history. In the Bahá'í Faith, however, the Lesser Covenant was put into writing in Bahá'u'lláh's will.

What does the Lesser Covenant cover in the Bahá'í Faith?

Bahá'u'lláh laid out His covenant in clear, written form, appointing 'Abdu'l-Bahá as His successor, the Center of the Covenant, to whom all believers should turn. 'Abdu'l-Bahá, in turn, wrote His own will, appointing Shoghi Effendi as Guardian and simultaneously promising that when the Universal House of Justice, the governing institution originally anticipated by Bahá'u'lláh, was elected, it would be blessed with divine guidance and protection.

AN OUTLINE OF THE LESSER COVENANT IN FOUR EASY STEPS

- 1892: Bahá'u'lláh outlined provisions for the eventual establishment of a House of Justice, but there were not enough Bahá'ís to support such an institution at that time, so in His will, He appointed 'Abdu'l-Bahá as the Center of the Covenant, to whom all the Bahá'ís of that time should turn.
- 1921: 'Abdu'l-Bahá, in His will, appointed Shoghi Effendi as the Guardian of the Bahá'í Faith and promised divine blessings for the Universal House of Justice when it was finally elected.
- 1953: Shoghi Effendi created a ten-year plan for the Bahá'ís of the world and indi-

cated that plans to follow this one would be overseen by the Universal House of Justice.

- 1963: Shoghi Effendi died in 1957, but the Bahá'ís of the world carried out the rest of the ten-year plan and, at its end, elected the first Universal House of Justice.

What is the role of an individual Bahá'í in the Lesser Covenant?

Bahá'ís are expected to follow the guidance of those who are appointed or elected. At one time, this meant obedience to the appointed Center of the Covenant, 'Abdu'l-Bahá. The parents of the author of this book, for instance, were alive during the Guardianship of Shoghi Effendi and consequently followed his guidance. Today, obedience to the provisions of the Covenant of Bahá'u'lláh means acknowledging the Universal House of Justice as the central authority of the Bahá'í Faith.

"As to the most great characteristic of the revelation of Bahá'u'lláh, a specific teaching not given by any of the Prophets of the past: It is the ordination and appointment of the Center of the Covenant." 'Abdu'l-Bahá, *The Promulgation of Universal Peace,* p. 642.

With what words did Bahá'u'lláh ask the Bahá'ís to turn to 'Abdu'l-Bahá for guidance in 1892?

"Consider that which We have revealed in Our Most Holy Book: 'When the ocean of My presence hath ebbed and the Book of My Revelation is ended, turn your faces toward Him Whom God hath purposed, Who hath branched from this Ancient Root.' The object of this sacred verse is none other except the Most Mighty Branch ['Abdu'l-Bahá]. Thus have We graciously revealed unto you our potent Will, and I am verily the Gracious, the All-Powerful. . . . Let not the means of order be made the cause of confusion and the instrument of union an occasion for discord." Bahá'u'lláh, *Tablets of Bahá'u'lláh,* pp. 221–22.

How did 'Abdu'l-Bahá's Will and Testament describe the authority of Shoghi Effendi as Guardian in 1921?

"The sacred and youthful branch, the Guardian of the Cause of God, as well as the Universal House of Justice to be universally elected and established, are both under the care and protection of the Abhá Beauty, under the shelter and unerring guidance of the Exalted One (may my life be offered up for them both). Whatsoever they decide is of God. Whoso obeyeth him not, neither obeyeth them, hath not obeyed God, whoso rebelleth against him and against them hath rebelled against God; whoso opposeth him hath opposed God; whoso contendeth with them hath contended with God; whoso disputeth with him hath disputed with God; whoso denieth him hath denied God; whoso disbelieveth in him hath disbelieved in God; whoso deviateth, separateth himself and turneth aside from him hath in truth deviated, separated himself and turned aside from God. May the wrath, the fierce indignation, the vengeance of God rest upon him! The mighty stronghold shall remain impregnable and safe through obedience to him who is the Guardian of the Cause of God." 'Abdu'l-Bahá, *Will and Testament of 'Abdu'l-Bahá*, p. 11.

Was there another Guardian after Shoghi Effendi?

No. Shoghi Effendi died in 1957 without naming a successor. 'Abdu'l-Bahá had indicated that such an appointment would have to be made from a descendant of the family, preferably the firstborn. However, Shoghi Effendi and his wife had no children and all of the other male branches of Bahá'u'lláh's family who might otherwise have been eligible had already become disobedient to the Covenant by attempting to seize power for themselves. Thus it was impossible to have a second Guardian.

Because Bahá'u'lláh and 'Abdu'l-Bahá had both anticipated the day when it would be time to elect a Universal House of Justice, the Hands of the Cause of God announced that this would take place as the culmination of the ten-year plan, in 1963. The Hands also took the selfless step of asking the worldwide Baha'i community to leave them free to carry out their duties as Hands of the Cause of God.

If there is no Guardian, how does the institution of the Guardianship still exist?

The institution of the Guardianship still exists in the form of all the writings of Shoghi Effendi, and it continues to be a source of authoritative guidance to individual believers as well as the Universal House of Justice.

How does 'Abdu'l-Bahá describe the authority that the Universal House of Justice would have when it was elected?

The Universal House of Justice, which is described as being "freed from all error," cannot change laws already given by Bahá'u'lláh, but it has the power to decide on matters that were not specifically mentioned in Bahá'u'lláh's writings. It also has the power to change any previous decisions it has made so that it can respond appropriately to the needs of the time:

"Unto the Most Holy Book [the Kitáb-i-Aqdas, written by Bahá'u'lláh] every one must turn, and all that is not expressly recorded therein must be referred to the Universal House of Justice. That which this body, whether unanimously or by a majority doth carry, that is verily the truth and the purpose of God Himself. Whoso doth deviate therefrom is verily of them that love discord, hath shown forth malice, and turned away from the Lord of the Covenant." 'Abdu'l-Bahá, *Will and Testament of 'Abdu'l-Bahá,* pp. 19–20.

". . . the House of Justice which God hath ordained as the source of all good and freed from all error . . ." 'Abdu'l-Bahá, *Will and Testament of 'Abdu'l-Bahá,* p. 14.

"It is incumbent upon these members (of the Universal House of Justice) to gather in a certain place and deliberate upon all problems which have caused difference, questions that are obscure and matters that are not expressly recorded in the Book. Whatsoever they decide has the same effect as the Text itself. Inasmuch as the House of Justice hath power to enact laws that are not expressly recorded in the Book and bear upon daily transactions, so also it hath power to repeal the same. Thus for example, the House of Justice enacteth today a certain law and enforceth it, and a hundred years hence, circumstances having profoundly changed and the conditions having altered, another House of Justice will then have power, according to the exigencies of the time, to alter that law. This it can do because these laws form no part of the divine explicit Text. The House of Justice is both the initiator and the abrogator of its own laws." 'Abdu'l-Bahá, *Will and Testament of 'Abdu'l-Bahá,* p. 20.

What does 'Abdu'l-Bahá mean when he describes the House of Justice as "freed from error?"

He means that God will grant the Universal House of Justice protection from error though the bounty of conferred infallibility. He also explains that there are two kinds of infallibility, essential infallibility that is only possessed by the Manifestations of God, and conferred infallibility that is a gift from God:

"Essential infallibility is peculiar to the supreme Manifestation, for it is His essential requirement, and an essential requirement cannot be separated from the thing itself. The rays are the essential necessity of the sun and are inseparable from it. Knowledge is an essential necessity of God and is inseparable from Him . . .

But acquired infallibility is not a natural necessity; on the contrary, it is a ray of the bounty of infallibility which shines from the Sun of Reality upon hearts, and grants a share and portion of itself to souls. Although these souls have not essential infallibility, still they are under the protection of God—that is to say, God preserves them from error. . . . If God did not protect them from error, their error would cause believing souls to fall into error, and thus the foundation of the Religion of God would be overturned, which would not be fitting nor worthy of God. . . . For instance, the Universal House of Justice, if it be established under the necessary conditions—with members elected from all the people—that House of Justice will be under the protection and unerring guidance of God. If that House of Justice shall decide unanimously, or by a majority, upon any question not mentioned in the Book, that decision and command will be guarded from mistake. Now the members of the House of Justice have not, individually, essential infallibility; but the body of the House of Justice is under the protection and unerring guidance of God; this is called conferred infallibility." 'Abdu'l-Bahá, *Some Answered Questions,* pp. 171–73.

What kind of election system was outlined by 'Abdu'l-Bahá for the Universal House of Justice?

The members of all of the National Spiritual Assemblies in the world (nine people per assembly) cast secret ballots to elect the members of the Universal House of Justice:

". . . in all countries a secondary House of Justice (a National Spiritual Assembly) must be instituted, and these secondary Houses of Justice must elect the members of the Universal one." 'Abdu'l-Bahá, *Will and Testament of 'Abdu'l-Bahá,* p. 14.

When was the Universal House of Justice first elected?

The first election took place in 1963. As anticipated by Bahá'u'lláh, the Universal House of Justice immediately became the consummate authority in all the affairs of the Bahá'í community. Thus the Bahá'í Faith remained united through what has historically been the most critical period of a religion's history—the vulnerable first century of its existence.

Turn to chapter 13 for more details about what the Universal House of Justice is and how it operates.

How does 'Abdu'l-Bahá describe the Lesser Covenant of Bahá'u'lláh?

So firm and mighty is this Covenant, that from the beginning of time until the present day no religious Dispensation hath produced its like.

'Abdu'l-Bahá, cited in Shoghi Effendi, *God Passes By*, p. 375.

What are some other things 'Abdu'l-Bahá said about the Covenant?

"'It is indubitably clear,' He, furthermore, has stated, 'that the pivot of the oneness of mankind is nothing else but the power of the Covenant.' 'Know thou,' He has written, 'that the *Sure Handle* mentioned from the foundation of the world in the Books, the Tablets and the Scriptures of old is naught else but the Covenant and Testament.' And again: 'The lamp of the Covenant is the light of the world, and the words traced by the Pen of the Most High a limitless ocean.' 'The Lord, the All-Glorified,' He has moreover declared, 'hath, beneath the shade of the Tree of Anísá (Tree of Life), made a new Covenant and established a great Testament. . . . Hath such a Covenant been established in any previous Dispensation, age, period or century? Hath such a Testament, set down by the Pen of the Most High, ever been witnessed? No, by God!'" Shoghi Effendi, quoting 'Abdu'l-Bahá, *God Passes By*, pp. 375–76.

"The power of the Covenant is as the heat of the sun which quickeneth and promoteth the development of all created things on earth. The light of the Covenant, in like manner, is the educator of the minds, the spirits, the hearts and souls of men." 'Abdu'l-Bahá, cited in Shoghi Effendi, *God Passes By*, p. 376.

What effect does the Covenant have on humanity?

"Today, every wise, vigilant and foresighted person is awakened, and to him are unveiled the mysteries of the future which show that nothing save the power of the Covenant is able to stir and move the heart of humanity, just as the New and Old Testaments propounded throughout all regions the Cause of Christ and were the pulsating power in the body of the human world." 'Abdu'l-Bahá, *Selections from the Writings of 'Abdu'l-Bahá*, no. 189.1.

How does the Covenant protect the unity of the Bahá'í Faith?

"The purpose of the Blessed Beauty in entering into this Covenant and Testament was to gather all existent beings around one point so that the thoughtless souls, who in every cycle and generation have been the cause of dissension, may not undermine the Cause. He hath, therefore, commanded that whatever emanateth from the Centre of the Covenant is right and is under His protection and favour, while all else is error." 'Abdu'l-Bahá, *Selections from the Writings of 'Abdu'l-Bahá,* no. 183.3.

"Today no power can conserve the oneness of the Bahá'í world save the Covenant of God. . . . It is evident that the axis of the oneness of the world of humanity is the power of the Covenant and nothing else." 'Abdu'l-Bahá, *Tablets of the Divine Plan,* p. 51.

Why is it the duty of a Bahá'í to obey the Covenant?

"To accept the Prophet of God in His time and to abide by His bidding are the two essential, inseparable duties which each soul was created to fulfill. One exercises these twin duties by one's own choice, an act constituting the highest expression of the free will with which

every human being has been endowed by an all-loving Creator.

"The vehicle in this resplendent Age for the practical fulfillment of these duties is the Covenant of Bahá'u'lláh; it is, indeed, the potent instrument by which individual belief in Him is translated into constructive deeds. The Covenant comprises divinely conceived arrangements necessary to preserve the organic unity of the Cause. It therefore engenders a motivating power which, as the beloved Master tells us, 'like unto the artery, beats and pulsates in the body of the world.' 'It is indubitably clear,' He asserts, 'that the pivot of the oneness of mankind is nothing else but the power of the Covenant.' Through it the meaning of the Word, both in theory and practice, is made evident in the life and work of 'Abdu'l-Bahá, the appointed Interpreter, the perfect Exemplar, the Center of the Covenant. Through it the processes of the Administrative Order—'this unique, this wondrous System'—are made to operate." The Universal House of Justice, *Individual Rights and Freedoms,* pp. 4–5.

What does it mean to break the Covenant?

"When a person declares his acceptance of Bahá'u'lláh as a Manifestation of God he becomes a party to the Covenant and accepts the totality of His Revelation. If he then . . . attacks Bahá'u'lláh or the Central Institution of the Faith he violates the Covenant. If this happens every effort is made to help that person to see the illogicality and error of his actions, but if he persists he must, in accordance with the instructions of Bahá'u'lláh Himself, be shunned as a Covenant-breaker." Letter from the Universal House of Justice to an individual believer, dated March 23, 1975.

What is an example of Covenant-breaking?

During the years between Shoghi Effendi's death and the election of Universal House of Justice, Mason Remey, a Hand of the Cause, came to believe that he should be named the second Guardian of the Bahá'í Faith because of his position as president of the International Bahá'í Council, a body that had been appointed to assist the Guardian in several ways, including that of functioning as secretariat.

Remey's claim had no basis in any of Shoghi Effendi's documents and was also clearly counter to 'Abdu'l-Bahá's Will and Testament. A scattering of people accepted the claim and they, along with Mason Remey, were judged to be Covenant-breakers. Mason Remey died in 1974,

leaving behind a few followers, several of whom put forth contending claims of leadership. Remnants of those groups still exist, but they are not considered to be part of the Bahá'í community.

Is someone who resigns from the Bahá'í Faith a Covenant-breaker?

No. Any individual who recognizes Bahá'u'-lláh as the Manifestation of God and embraces His Faith but later changes his mind and withdraws his membership is not a Covenant-breaker. Bahá'ís will respect such a decision and remain friends with that person.

Can other challenges to the Bahá'í Covenant be expected?

"The tests of every dispensation are in direct proportion to the greatness of the Cause, and as heretofore such a manifest Covenant, written by the Supreme Pen, hath not been entered upon, the tests are proportionately severe." 'Abdu'l-Bahá, *Selections from the Writings of 'Abdu'l-Bahá*, no. 185.1.

Can the Covenant survive these tests?

The Hand of Omnipotence hath established His Revelation upon an unassailable, an enduring foundation. Storms of human strife are powerless to undermine its basis, nor will men's fanciful theories succeed in damaging its structure.
Bahá'u'lláh, cited in Shoghi Effendi, *World Order of Bahá'u'lláh,* p. 109.

How do the forces of the universe serve the Covenant?

"Today, the Lord of Hosts is the defender of the Covenant, the forces of the Kingdom protect it, heavenly souls tender their services, and heavenly angels promulgate and spread it broadcast. If it is considered with insight, it will be seen that all the forces of the universe, in the last analysis serve the Covenant." 'Abdu'l-Bahá, *Selections from the Writings of 'Abdu'l-Bahá,* no. 192.1.

O ye beloved of the Lord! The greatest of all things is the protection of the True Faith of God, the preservation of His Law, the safeguarding of His Cause and service unto His Word. 'Abdu'l-Bahá, *Will and Testament of 'Abdu'l-Bahá,* p. 4.

CHAPTER 13

The Administrative Order

Bahá'u'lláh's plan for uniting the hearts of humankind and bringing peace to the world is referred to as the "World Order of Bahá'u'lláh." Bahá'ís believe it is destined eventually to be embraced by most people. Its nucleus is the present Bahá'í Administrative Order.

Bahá'u'lláh revealed its guiding principles, established its institutions, and ordained its operations and functions in the Kitáb-i-Aqdas (the Most Holy Book), the Tablet of Carmel and the Kitáb-i-'Ahd (The Book of the Covenant).

How has the Administrative Order been developed since the death of Bahá'u'lláh?

'Abdu'l-Bahá reaffirmed the basis of the Administrative Order and supplemented its principles. Shoghi Effendi guided the growth of the young institutions and further developed their working guidelines. The Universal House of Justice is now the continuing source of authority and direction.

What is the purpose of the Administrative Order?

The purpose of the Administrative Order is to establish the Kingdom of God on earth by gradually bringing about and maintaining an entirely new mode of community life built on love, unity, and service to God.

What are the two groups of administrative institutions in the Bahá'í Faith?

ELECTED

The elected bodies in charge of governing are the Universal House of Justice, National Spiritual Assemblies, Regional Bahá'í Councils, and Local Spiritual Assemblies.

APPOINTED

The appointed bodies whose function is advisory include the International Teaching Center plus the Continental Boards of Counselors and their auxiliary boards.

Who holds authority and power?

The authority to make decisions lies in the hands of the freely elected governing bodies functioning at the local, national, regional, and international levels, but the power to carry out these decisions resides with the individual believer.

The purpose of the appointed bodies, whose members serve for limited terms, is to offer assistance in issues of moral leadership as well as protection and propagation of the Bahá'í community, but this is solely in an advisory capacity. They do not possess any administrative authority.

What is the value of the Bahá'í Administrative Order?

"In a world the structure of whose political and social institutions is impaired, whose vision is befogged, whose conscience is bewildered, whose religious sys-

tems have become anemic and lost their virtue, this healing Agency, this leavening Power, this cementing Force, intensely alive and all-pervasive, has been taking shape, is crystallizing into institutions, is mobilizing its forces, and is preparing for the spiritual conquest and the complete redemption of mankind. Though the society which incarnates its ideals be small, and its direct and tangible benefits as yet inconsiderable, yet the potentialities with which it has been endowed, and through which it is destined to regenerate the individual and rebuild a broken world, are incalculable." Shoghi Effendi, *World Order of Bahá'u'lláh,* p. 195.

What is unique about the Bahá'í Administrative Order?

"[T]his Administrative Order is fundamentally different from anything that any Prophet has previously established, inasmuch as Bahá'u'lláh has Himself revealed its principles, established its institutions, appointed the person to interpret His Word and conferred the necessary authority on the body designed to supplement and apply His legislative ordinances. Therein lies the secret of its strength, its fundamental distinction, and the guarantee against disintegration and schism. Nowhere in the sacred scriptures of any of the world's religious systems, nor even in the writings of the Inaugurator of the Bábí Dispensation, do we find provisions establishing a covenant or providing for an administrative order that compare in scope and authority with those that lie at the very basis of the Bahá'í Dispensation." Shoghi Effendi, *World Order of Bahá'u'lláh,* p. 145.

The Universal House of Justice

What is the Universal House of Justice?

The Universal House of Justice is the supreme governing and legislative body of the Bahá'í Faith. The membership is at present fixed at nine. The members are elected every five years by the members of the National Spiritual Assemblies. The members reside in Haifa, Israel, and meet in the building on Mount Carmel known as the Seat of the Universal House of Justice.

What are the decision-making parameters for the Universal House of Justice?

The Universal House of Justice cannot change any of Bahá'u'lláh's laws. However, it has the power to enact laws that are not expressly recorded in the writings and it also has the power to repeal them later on as conditions change.

Why is obeying the Universal House of Justice similar to obeying God?

"[The Universal House of Justice is] under the care and protection of the Abhá Beauty [Bahá'u'lláh], under the shelter and unerring guidance of His Holiness, the Exalted One [the Báb]. . . . Whatsoever they decide is of God. Whoso obeyeth him not, neither obeyeth them, hath not obeyed God; whoso rebelleth against him and against them hath rebelled against God; whoso opposeth him hath opposed God; whoso contendeth with them hath contended with God. . ." 'Abdu'l-Bahá, *Will and Testament of 'Abdu'l-Bahá,* p. 11.

Do both men and women serve on the Universal House of Justice?

"The House of Justice, however, according to the explicit text of the Law of God, is confined to men; this is for a wisdom of the Lord God's which will ere long be made manifest as clearly as the sun at high noon." 'Abdu'l-Bahá, *Selections from the Writings of 'Abdu'l-Bahá,* no. 38.4.

National Spiritual Assemblies

National Spiritual Assemblies, consisting of nine members, are elected annually by delegates that are themselves elected from among the adult membership of the Bahá'ís of that country. Any adult Bahá'í in good standing—woman or man—can be elected.

How did Shoghi Effendi describe National Assemblies?

". . . National Assemblies, the pivots round which all national undertakings must revolve . . . are empowered to direct, unify, coordinate and stimulate the activities of individuals as well as local Assemblies within their jurisdiction. Resting on the broad base of organized local communities, themselves pillars sustaining the institution which must be regarded as the apex of the Bahá'í Administrative Order, these Assemblies are elected, according to the principle of proportional representation, by delegates representative of Bahá'í local communities assembled at Convention during the period of the Riḍván Festival; are possessed of the necessary authority to enable them to insure the harmonious and efficient development of Bahá'í activity within their respective spheres; are freed from all direct responsibility for their policies and decisions to their electorates; are charged with the sacred duty of consulting the views, of inviting the recommendations and of securing the confidence and cooperation of the delegates and of acquainting them with their plans, problems and actions; and are supported by the resources of national funds to which all ranks of the faithful are urged to contribute." Shoghi Effendi, *God Passes By,* pp. 526–27.

When was the first National Spiritual Assembly elected?

'Abdu'l-Bahá made provisions for national assemblies in His Will and Testament, and the first one was elected in 1925: the National Spiritual Assembly of the Bahá'ís of the United States and Canada.

Regional Councils

Regional Councils are intermediary bodies between the Local and National Assemblies that provide a means for a rapid response to the needs of a specific region. Their primary focus is on fostering teaching work in a coordinated yet community-based manner.

Regional Councils were created by the Universal House of Justice and first elected in the United States in 1997. In the United States, there are ten Regional Councils. Each one has nine members who are elected annually by members of all the Local Spiritual Assemblies within its geographic area. Ties are decided by lot.

Local Spiritual Assemblies

A Local Spiritual Assembly is the administrative body of a local Bahá'í community. Its nine members are elected annually from among the believers in a community and serve for a period of one year. All adult believers (age 21 and over) in a community are eligible for election. The assembly elects its own officers for the year and meets as often as it finds necessary. The Local Assembly oversees the teaching and other work of the Bahá'í community, conducts marriages and funerals, and provides Bahá'í education for children and youth as well as classes for adults. It is responsible for seeing that the Nineteen Day Feast is held and that there are Holy Day observances. Those in difficulty may call upon it for advice, guidance, and assistance.

What are the duties of a Local Spiritual Assembly?

"Among the more salient objectives to be attained by the Local Spiritual Assembly in its process of development to full maturity are to act as a loving shepherd to the Bahá'í flock, promote unity and concord among the friends, direct the teaching work, protect the Cause of God, arrange for Feasts, Anniversaries and regular meetings of the community, familiarize the Bahá'ís with its plans, invite the community to offer its recommendations, promote the welfare of youth and children, and participate, as circumstances permit, in humanitarian activities. In its relationship to the individual believer, the Assembly should continuously invite and encourage him to study the Faith, to deliver its glorious message, to live in accordance with its teachings, to contribute freely and regularly to the Fund, to participate in community activities, and to seek refuge in the Assembly for advice and help, when needed." The Universal House of Justice, letter to the National Spiritual Assembly of Bolivia, dated July 30, 1972.

Special Features of Spiritual Assemblies

How are Local and National Spiritual Assemblies different than other religious administrative bodies?

"The Spiritual Assemblies to be established in the Age of God, this holy century, have, it is indisputable, had neither peer nor likeness in the cycles gone before. For those assemblages that wielded power were based on the support of mighty leaders of men, while these Assemblies are based on the support of the Beauty of Abhá. The defenders and patrons of those other assemblages were either a prince, or a king, or a chief priest, or the mass of the people. But these Spiritual Assemblies have for their defender,

their supporter, their helper, their inspirer, the omnipotent Lord." 'Abdu'l-Bahá, *Selections from the Writings of 'Abdu'l-Bahá,* no. 40.2.

Will the role of Assemblies change with time?

Yes, the Universal House of Justice has indicated that the duties and functions of Assemblies will change as the Bahá'í Faith grows and matures.

"Local Spiritual Assemblies are at the present newly-born institutions, struggling for the most part to establish themselves both in the Bahá'í community and in the world. They are as yet only embryos of the majestic institutions ordained by Bahá'u'lláh in His Writings." The Universal House of Justice, in *Lights of Guidance,* no. 149.

The Distinctive Nature of Bahá'í Elections

An extremely important and sacred part of the Bahá'í Administrative Order is the distinctive nature of elections. There are no nominations, no running for office, no campaigning, and no discussion of personalities. The list of those who can be elected consists of all the adult Bahá'ís in a particular community/area/country (with the exception of those whose voting rights may have been removed—see chapter 11 for more information).

At election time, adult Bahá'ís come together in a spirit of unity and friendliness (those unable to attend may vote by mail). After prayers asking God for His guidance and aid, the believers vote by secret ballot. The nine people elected are those receiving the highest number of votes.

In case of a tie for the final place, if one of those tied belongs to a distinct minority within the community, he / she is automatically given the position. If not, a revote or lottery is used, depending on the body being elected.

The Institution of the Learned

"This Administrative Order consists, on the one hand, of a series of elected councils, universal, secondary and local, in which are vested legislative, executive and judicial powers over the Bahá'í community and, on the other, of eminent and devoted believers appointed for the specific purposes of protecting and propagating the Faith of Bahá'u'lláh under the guidance of the Head of that Faith.

"The Hands of the Cause of God, the Counselors and the members of the Auxiliary Boards fall within the definition of the *learned* given by the beloved Guardian. Thus they are all intimately interrelated and it is not incorrect to refer to the three ranks collectively as one institution. However, each is also a separate institution in itself." The Universal House of Justice, *Messages from the Universal House of Justice: 1968–1973,* pp. 91–92.

Hands of the Cause

Hands of the Cause were individuals appointed first by Bahá'u'lláh, then by 'Abdu'l-Bahá, and later by Shoghi Effendi. They were charged with specific duties, especially those of protecting and propagating the Bahá'í Faith. Shoghi Effendi referred to them as "Chief Stewards of Bahá'u'lláh's embryonic World Commonwealth."

After the death of Shoghi Effendi, the Hands of the Cause served as interim directors of the Bahá'í Faith. Under their direction, the Bahá'ís of the world completed a ten-year plan that had been inaugurated in 1953 by Shoghi Effendi and elected the first Universal House of Justice in 1963.

Based on 'Abdu'l-Bahá's description of the appointment of the Hands of the Cause as having to be done by a Guardian, the Universal House of Justice stated there could be no further appointments after Shoghi Effendi's passing. Instead, the functions of the Hands of the Cause in relation to protecting and propagating the Faith have been continued through the creation of the Continental Boards of Counselors and the establishment of an International Teaching Center. The last living Hand of the Cause died in 2007.

International Teaching Center

This institution was established in 1973 by the Universal House of Justice and is based in Haifa, Israel. Among its duties are that of gathering and analyzing information about the growth and consolidation of the Bahá'í Faith throughout the world, providing guidance and resources to the Continental Counsellors, and fostering the development of Bahá'í community life.

Continental Boards of Counselors

Boards of Counselors are appointed by the Universal House of Justice for terms of five years. Each board is assigned to a different continent with the responsibility of consulting and collaborating with National Spiritual Assemblies and keeping the International Teaching Center informed concerning the conditions of the Bahá'í Faith in that area. Counselors are not eligible for any elective office except the Universal House of Justice, in which case that person must resign from the board.

Auxiliary Boards

Auxiliary Boards for protection and for propagation are appointed by, and responsible to, the Continental Counselors for their area. Their role is not administrative but advisory, and they work closely with the communities to which they have been assigned. Their primary functions are advising, stimulating, and assisting Local Spiritual Assemblies, groups, and individual believers. If elected to a Spiritual Assembly, the member must choose between serving in that capacity or continuing as an Auxiliary Board member. Each Auxiliary Board member may appoint assistants to help with the work.

Training Institutes

In 1997, the Universal House of Justice introduced the concept of Training Institutes as a means by which new Bahá'ís and other interested individuals could systematically study the Bahá'í teachings and acquire the spiritual attitudes, skills, and capacities needed to foster the development of a peaceful and prosperous world. The institutes are organized at a regional level and are under the guidance of Regional Bahá'í Councils. Most of them use a community-based approach to education by relying on a network of local tutors who offer a series of courses, referred to as study circles. The courses generally include service components that lead participants into taking an active role in organizing children's classes, mentoring junior youth groups, hosting devotional gatherings, deepening new believers, introducing the Bahá'í Faith to those who have not heard of it, or being of service to humanity through some other avenue.

Spirituality and Administration

"Regarding the relationship of the Cause to the Administration, the Bahá'í Faith, as the Guardian himself has repeatedly and emphatically stated, cannot be confined to a mere system of organization, however elaborate in its features and universal in its scope it may be. Organization is only a means to the realization of its aims and ideals, and not an end in itself. To divorce the two, however, would be to mutilate the Cause itself, as they stand inseparably bound to each other, in very much the same relationship existing between the soul and body in the world of human existence." Letter written on behalf of Shoghi Effendi, in *Lights of Guidance,* no. 6.

Avoiding Partisan Politics

Bahá'ís do not join or maintain membership in a political party, though they may participate in civil political elections in a nonpartisan way. Voting in local and national elections can be done as long as there is no requirement to align with any party. Bahá'ís avoid discussing partisan politics. When political controversies arise, they assign no blame and take no sides. Instead, their focus is on creating unity and drawing people together through Bahá'u'lláh's teachings.

"We should not only take side with no political party, group or system actually in use, but we should also refuse to commit ourselves to any statement which may be interpreted as being sympathetic or antagonistic to any existing political organization or philosophy. The attitude of the Bahá'ís must be one of complete aloofness. They are neither for nor against any system of politics . . . due to certain basic con-siderations arising out of their teachings and of the administrative machinery of their Faith they prefer not to get entangled in political affairs." Letter written on behalf of Shoghi Effendi to an individual believer, dated March 2, 1934.

What is the wisdom of avoiding partisan politics?

"If the institutions of the Faith, God forbid, became involved in politics, the Bahá'ís would find themselves arousing antagonism instead of love. If they took one stand in one country, they would be bound to change the views of the people in other countries about the aims and purposes of the Faith. By becoming involved in political disputes, the Bahá'ís instead of changing the world or helping it, would themselves be lost and destroyed. The world situation is so confused and moral issues which were once clear have become so mixed up with selfish and battling factions, that the best way Bahá'ís can serve the highest interests of their country and the cause of true salvation for the world, is to sacrifice their political pursuits and affiliations and wholeheartedly and fully support the divine system of Bahá'u'lláh." The Universal House of Justice, in *Lights of Guidance,* no. 1449.

CHAPTER 14

Spiritual Practices of Everyday Life

Set before thine eyes God's unerring Balance and, as one standing in His Presence, weigh in that Balance thine actions every day, every moment of thy life.

Bahá'u'lláh, *Gleanings from the Writings of Bahá'u'lláh*, no. 141.12.

Prayer

The state of prayer is the best of conditions, for man is then associating with God. 'Abdu'l-Bahá, *Selections from the Writings of 'Abdu'l-Bahá,* no. 172.1.

Why is prayer necessary?

Prayer, as described in the Bahá'í writings, is an indispensable element of spiritual growth and insight:

"I bear witness, O my God, that Thou hast created me to know Thee and to worship Thee." Bahá'u'lláh, in *Bahá'í Prayers,* p. 4.

"Whoso reciteth, in the privacy of his chamber, the verses revealed by God, the scattering angels of the Almighty shall scatter abroad the fragrance of the words uttered by his mouth, and shall cause the heart of every righteous man to throb. Though he may, at first, remain unaware of its effect, yet the virtue of the grace vouchsafed unto him must needs sooner or later exercise its influence upon his soul." Bahá'u'lláh, in *Bahá'í Prayers,* p. iii.

". . . gifts of the spirit are received through prayer, meditation, study of the Holy Utterances and service to the Cause of God." Letter written on behalf of Shoghi Effendi to an individual believer, in *Lights of Guidance,* no. 247.

Are certain prayers obligatory?

It is obligatory to pray at least once a day, but Bahá'ís can choose which of three obligatory prayers revealed by Bahá'u'lláh they want to recite.

Before saying an obligatory prayer, ablutions are performed. This means washing the hands and face with water. It is easy to understand that the washing is a spiritual preparation and not just a physical action because even if one has just finished bathing, it is still necessary to perform the ablutions.

Specific instructions that accompany an obligatory prayer may include actions like standing, kneeling, or raising one's hands. Shoghi Effendi explained that the movements are symbols of an inner attitude. The time of day set for the two shorter prayers—morning, noon or evening—refers respectively to the intervals between sunrise and noon, between noon and sunset, and from sunset to two hours after sunset. The long obligatory prayer should be said once in twenty-four hours, at whatever time one chooses.

Is there a certain direction to face during prayer?

While saying an obligatory prayer, one faces toward the place where Bahá'u'lláh is buried, in Bahjí, Israel. This is called the Qiblih (Point of Adoration).

For all other prayers, one may face in any direction.

Do obligatory prayers have special power?

". . . the obligatory prayers are by their very nature of greater effectiveness and are endowed with a greater power than the non-obligatory ones, and as such are essential." Letter written on behalf of Shoghi Effendi, in *Lights of Guidance,* no. 2160.

When should other prayers be said?

"At the dawn of every day he should commune with God, and with all his soul persevere in the quest of his Beloved. He should consume every wayward thought with the flame of His loving mention, and, with the swiftness of lightning, pass by all else save Him." Bahá'u'lláh, Kitáb-i-Íqán, ¶214.

"Prayer verily bestoweth life, particularly when offered in private and at times, such as midnight, when freed from daily cares." 'Abdu'l-Bahá, *Selections from the Writings of 'Abdu'l-Bahá,* no. 172.1.

Can prayers be set to music?

Yes, Bahá'ís are free to set the prayers and other Bahá'í writings to music as long as it is done with a sense of reverence.

Is there a need for privacy during prayer?

"Whoso reciteth, in the privacy of his chamber, the verses revealed by God, the scattering angels of the Almighty shall scatter abroad the fragrance of the words uttered by his mouth, and shall cause the heart of every righteous man to throb. Though he may, at first, remain unaware of its effect, yet the virtue of the grace vouchsafed unto him must needs sooner or later exercise its influence upon his soul. Thus have the mysteries of the Revelation of God been decreed by virtue of the Will of Him Who is the Source of power and wisdom." Bahá'u'lláh, *Gleanings from the Writings of Bahá'u'lláh,* no. 136.2.

"The reason why privacy hath been enjoined in moments of devotion is this, that thou mayest give thy best attention to the remembrance of God, that thy heart may at all times be animated with His Spirit, and not be shut out as by a veil from thy Best Beloved. Let not thy tongue pay lip service in praise of God while thy heart be not attuned to the exalted summit of Glory, and the Focal Point of communion." The Báb, *Selections from the Writings of the Báb,* no. 3:21:1.

"It is striking how private and personal the most fundamental spiritual exercises of prayer and meditation are in the Faith. Bahá'ís do, of course, have meetings for devotions . . . but the daily obligatory prayers are ordained to be said in the privacy of one's chamber, and meditation on the Teachings is, likewise a private individual activity. . ." The Universal House of Justice, in *Lights of Guidance,* no. 1836.

Should a family pray together?

". . . the members [of a family] should feel responsible for making the collective life of the family a spiritual reality, animated by divine love and inspired by the ennobling principles of the Faith. To achieve this purpose, the reading of the Sacred Writings and prayers should ideally become a daily family activity." The Universal House of Justice, in *Lights of Guidance,* no. 764.

Should we pray for our parents?

"It is seemly that the servant should, after each prayer, supplicate God to bestow mercy and forgiveness upon his parents." The Báb, *Selections from the Writings of the Báb,* no. 3:22:1.

Do Bahá'ís generally fold their hands or bow their head while praying?

There are no set forms for how one should pray, so it is not necessary to fold hands or adopt any other special posture (except as directed in the obligatory prayers). A respectful attitude is expected, of course, but how this is expressed can vary from culture to culture. In the United States, Bahá'ís commonly sit quietly while praying, and people often bow their heads as a sign of reverence. Parents sometimes teach their children to cross their arms and bow their heads while listening to a prayer to help them learn how to concentrate.

Do Bahá'ís usually pray directly from Bahá'í scripture or do they use their own words?

Prayers written by Bahá'u'lláh, the Báb, and 'Abdu'l-Bahá are revered as being endowed with great spiritual power and meaning, which is why most Bahá'ís prefer to use them. Individuals are also free to pray privately in their own heartfelt words.

Do Bahá'ís pray before meals?

Shoghi Effendi asked Bahá'ís not to make a practice of saying grace before a meal because this is not something enjoined by Bahá'u'lláh (*Lights of Guidance*, no. 1501). Bahá'ís come from all sorts of different races and religions, which means that almost everyone who joins the Bahá'í Faith faces the challenge of letting go of certain previous traditions.

What should we ask for when praying?

"The true worshipper, while praying, should endeavour not so much to ask God to fulfill his wishes and desires, but rather to adjust these and make them conform to the Divine Will. Only through such an attitude can one derive that feeling of inner peace and contentment which the power of prayer alone can confer." Letter written on behalf of Shoghi Effendi, in *The Compilation of Compilations vol. II*, no. 1768.

Are prayers answered?

". . . God will give to us when we ask Him. His mercy is all-encircling. But we ask for things which the divine wisdom does not desire for us, and there is no answer to our prayer. His wisdom does not sanction what we wish. We pray "O God! Make me wealthy!" If this prayer were universally answered, human affairs would be at a standstill. There would be none left to work in the streets, none to till the soil, none to build, none to run the trains. Therefore, it is evident that it would not be well for us if all prayers were answered. The affairs of the world would be interfered with, energies crippled and progress hindered. But whatever we ask for which is in accord with divine wisdom, God will answer." 'Abdu'l-Bahá, *The Promulgation of Universal Peace*, pp. 345–46.

Pray for strength. It will be given to you, no matter how difficult the conditions.
'Abdu'l-Bahá, *The Compilation of Compilations, vol. I*, no. 308.

Are prayers always said in words?

". . . Prayer need not be in words, but rather in thought and action. But if this love and this desire are lacking, it is useless to try to force them. Words without love mean nothing. If a person talks to you as an unpleasant duty, finding neither love nor enjoyment in the meeting, do you wish to converse with him?" 'Abdu'l-Bahá, in *The Compilation of Compilations, vol. II*, no. 236.

Reciting the verses of God

"Recite ye the verses of God every morn and eventide. Whoso faileth to recite them hath not been faithful to the Covenant of God and His Testament." Bahá'u'lláh, Kitáb-i-Aqdas, ¶149.

"[an essential requisite for spiritual growth is] regular reading of the Sacred Scriptures, specifically at least each morning and evening, with reverence, attention and thought." The Universal House of Justice, *Messages from the Universal House of Justice 1963–1986*, no. 375.5.

What are the verses of God?

The verses of God (the ones that should be recited every morning and eve) are primarily the writings of Bahá'u'lláh, although Bahá'ís may also use the writings of the Báb (Bahá'u'lláh, Kitáb-i-Aqdas, note 165, and a letter from the Universal House of Justice to an individual believer, dated November 30, 1995).

Can recitation be done with others?

"Gather ye together with the utmost joy and fellowship and recite the verses revealed by the merciful Lord. By so doing the doors to true knowledge will be opened to your inner beings, and ye then will feel your souls endowed with steadfastness and your hearts filled with radiant joy." Bahá'u'lláh, in *The Compilation of Compilations, vol. I*, no. 364.

What is the effect of prayer / reading / recitation?

"Intone, O My Servant, the verses of God that have been received by thee, as intoned by them who have drawn nigh unto Him, that the sweetness of thy melody may kindle thine own soul, and attract the hearts of all men. Whoso reciteth, in the privacy of his chamber, the verses revealed by God, the scattering angels of the Almighty shall scatter abroad the fragrance of the words uttered by his mouth, and shall cause the heart of every righteous man to throb." Bahá'u'lláh, *Gleanings from the Writings of Bahá'u'lláh*, no. 136.2.

"It behoveth us one and all to recite day and night both the Persian and Arabic Hidden Words, to pray fervently and supplicate tearfully that we may be enabled to conduct ourselves in accordance with these divine counsels.

These holy Words have not been revealed to be heard but to be practiced." 'Abdu'l-Bahá, in *The Compilation of Compilations, vol. I,* no. 395.

Is it a good idea to memorize some of the Bahá'í writings?

"From the texts of the wondrous, heavenly Scriptures they should memorize phrases and passages bearing on various instances, so that in the course of their speech they may recite divine verses whenever the occasion demandeth it, inasmuch as these holy verses are the most potent elixir, the greatest and mightiest talisman." Bahá'u'lláh, *Tablets of Bahá'u'lláh,* p. 200.

"We should memorize the Hidden Words, follow the exhortations of the Incomparable Lord, and conduct ourselves in a manner which befitteth our servitude at the threshold of the one true God." 'Abdu'l-Bahá, in *The Compilation of Compilations, vol. I,* no. 396.

Meditation

"Meditate profoundly, that the secret of things unseen may be revealed unto you, that you may inhale the sweetness of a spiritual and imperishable fragrance . . ." Bahá'u'lláh, Kitáb-i-Íqán, ¶8.

What is the purpose of meditation?

"Bahá'u'lláh says there is a sign (from God) in every phenomenon: the sign of the intellect is contemplation and the sign of contemplation is silence, because it is impossible for a man to do two things at one time—he cannot both speak and meditate.

It is an axiomatic fact that while you meditate you are speaking with your own spirit. In that state of mind you put certain questions to your spirit and the spirit answers: the light breaks forth and the reality is revealed. . . .

Meditation is the key for opening the doors of mysteries. . . .

The meditative faculty is akin to the mirror; if you put it before earthly objects it will reflect them. Therefore if the spirit of man is contemplating earthly subjects he will be informed of these.

But if you turn the mirror of your spirits heavenwards, the heavenly constellations and the rays of the Sun of Reality will be reflected in your hearts, and the virtues of the Kingdom will be obtained." 'Abdu'l-Bahá, *Paris Talks,* nos. 54.8–18.

Is there a certain way to meditate?

"There are no set forms of meditation prescribed in the teachings, no plan, as such, for inner development. The friends are urged—nay enjoined—to pray, and they also should meditate, but the manner of doing the latter is left entirely to the individual." Shoghi Effendi, in *Lights of Guidance,* no. 1482.

The Greatest Name

Bahá is a special name of God used by Bahá'u'lláh and designated as God's Most Great Name (or Greatest Name). Bahá means *glory*, *splendor* or *light*. Bahá'u'lláh used it as part of His own title, *the Glory of God*.

How is the Greatest Name used?

The phrase *Alláh-u-Abhá* is a version of the Greatest Name that can be used as a greeting. It can be translated as *God the All-Glorious*.

There is also an invocation based on the Most Great Name: *Ya Baha'u'l-Abhá,* which, when translated, means *O Thou Glory of Glories* (*Letters from the Guardian to Australia and New Zealand,* p. 41).

When should the Greatest Name be recited?

"It hath been ordained that every believer in God, the Lord of Judgment, shall, each day, having washed his hands and then his face, seat himself and repeat 'Alláh-u-Abhá' ninety-five times." Bahá'u'lláh, Kitáb-i-Aqdas, ¶18.

Note: If one has already washed hands and face for an obligatory prayer, it is not necessary to do it again before the recitation. One can face any direction while reciting the Greatest Name.

Does reciting mean saying out loud?

Reciting the Greatest Name simply means to repeat it over and over, silently or out loud or even set to music.

How are calligraphic forms of the Greatest Name used?

Artists have rendered the phrase *Yá-Bahá'u'l-Abhá* (translated as either *God the All-Glorious* or *O Glory of Glories*) in flowing calligraphy that can be used in decorative wall hangings in homes and Bahá'í Centers or placed on jewelry.

A simplified version of the Greatest Name can be engraved on a ring. The Arabic letters are put together in a way that creates three horizontal lines. The top line represents the world of God, the middle line is the world of His Manifestations, and the bottom line is the human world. The vertical stroke connecting the three horizontal lines links the divine Messengers to God as well as to the world of man. The two stars represent the twin Messengers for this age, the Báb and Bahá'u'lláh.

The Number 9

Why are Bahá'ís so fond of nine-pointed stars?

A nine-pointed star is often used as a symbol because the number *nine* has great significance in the Bahá'í revelation. It was nine years after the announcement of the Báb that Bahá'u'lláh received an intimation of His mission. Nine, as the highest single-digit number, also symbolizes completeness and unity, thus reflecting the central teachings of the Bahá'í Faith.

Why do Bahá'í temples have nine sides?

Nine-sided temples, with doors facing all parts of the world, symbolize unity and invite people from every religion, race, and ethnic background to enter.

Studying the Sacred Writings

Why is it important to study Bahá'u'lláh's writings?

Immerse yourselves in the ocean of My words, that ye may unravel its secrets, and discover all the pearls of wisdom that lie hid in its depths.

Bahá'u'lláh, Kitáb-i-Aqdas, ¶182.

". . . the reading of the scriptures and holy books is for no other purpose except to enable the reader to apprehend their meaning and unravel their innermost mysteries. Otherwise reading, without understanding, is of no abiding profit unto man." Bahá'u'lláh, Kitáb-i-Íqán, ¶185.

"My holy, My divinely ordained Revelation may be likened unto an ocean in whose depths are concealed innumerable pearls of great price, of surpassing luster. It is the duty of every seeker to bestir himself and strive to attain the shores of this ocean, so that he may, in proportion to the eagerness of his search and the efforts he hath exerted, partake of such benefits as have been preordained in God's irrevocable and hidden Tablets." Bahá'u'lláh, *Gleanings from the Writings of Bahá'u'lláh,* no. 153.5.

"To strive to obtain a more adequate understanding of the significance of Bahá'u'lláh's stupendous Revelation must, it is my unalterable conviction, remain the first obligation and the object of the constant endeavor of each one of its loyal adherents." Shoghi Effendi, *World Order of Bahá'u'lláh,* p. 100.

What can be discovered by studying Bahá'í scripture?

"If you read the utterances of Bahá'u'lláh and 'Abdu'l-Bahá with selflessness and care and concentrate upon them, you will discover truths unknown to you before and will obtain an insight into the problems that have baffled the great thinkers of the world." Letter written on behalf of Shoghi Effendi, in *The Compilation of Compilations, vol. II,* no. 1270.

Is it possible to overdo praying, reciting and meditating?

"Pride not yourselves on much reading of the verses or on a multitude of pious acts by night and day; for were a man to read a single verse with joy and radiance it would be better for him than to read with lassitude all the Holy Books of God, the Help in Peril, the Self-Subsisting. Read ye the sacred verses in such measure that ye be not overcome by languor and despondency. Lay not upon your souls that which will weary them and weigh them down, but rather what will lighten and uplift them, so that they may soar on the wings of the Divine verses towards the Dawning-place of His manifest signs; this will draw you nearer to God, did ye but comprehend." Bahá'u'lláh, Kitáb-i-Aqdas, ¶149.

Are prayer, meditation, and study enough to make me a spiritual person?

No. Action, based on insights garnered during prayer and meditation and study, is also essential:

"Read ye The Hidden Words, ponder the inner meanings thereof, and act in accord therewith." 'Abdu'l-Bahá, *Selections from the Writings of 'Abdu'l-Bahá,* no. 17.3.

"Act by day and night according to the teachings and counsels and admonitions of Bahá'u'lláh." 'Abdu'l-Bahá, *Selections from the Writings of 'Abdu'l-Bahá,* no. 64.3.

"Prayer and meditation are very important factors in deepening the spiritual life of the individual, but with them must go action and example, as these are the tangible results of the former. Both are essential." Shoghi Effendi, in *Lights of Guidance,* no. 1483.

Daily Checklist

- Pray and read / recite in the morning

- Say an obligatory prayer and repeat the Greatest Name

- Study the Bahá'í writings

- Take time to meditate

- Strive to put Bahá'u'lláh's teachings into action

- Pray and read / recite in the evening

CHAPTER 15

A New Rhythm of Life

"Well is it with him who in every Dispensation recognizeth the Purpose of God for that Dispensation, and is not deprived therefrom by turning his gaze towards the things of the past." The Báb, *Selections from the Writings of the Báb,* no. 3:34:2.

The Bahá'í Calendar: a New Rhythm of Daily Life

The Bahá'í calendar was established by the Báb and was called the Badí (wondrous) calendar. It was later approved and refined by Bahá'u'lláh, although He left a few questions about its application to be decided by the Universal House of Justice.

What does a Bahá'í year look like?

A Bahá'í year is based on a solar year of 365 days, five hours and approximately fifty minutes. New Year's Day (Naw-Rúz) coincides with the spring equinox in the Northern Hemisphere and is celebrated on March 21. A year consists of nineteen months of nineteen days each, giving a total of 361 days. The extra days (intercalary days) are placed between the eighteenth and nineteenth month, yielding four days—or five in a leap year—when the festival of Ayyám-i-Há takes place.

The Bahá'í day runs from sunset to sunset. A Bahá'í week is the same length as the one in current use—seven days—but each day has been given a new name. The day of rest designated by 'Abdu'l-Bahá is Friday (*Lights of Guidance,* no. 372).

When did the Bahá'í calendar begin?

The years of the Bahá'í Era are counted from the new year that began on March 21, 1844, just a few weeks before the Declaration of the Báb. Thus the 169th year of the Bahá'í Era began on March 21, 2012.

When do Bahá'ís gather together to worship?

Bahá'ís worship at many times and places. For instance, they may pray with their families, neighbors, and friends. Or they may organize a devotional gathering that includes people of many faiths. They also participate in a monthly community gathering known as the nineteen-day feast, which takes place on the first day of each Bahá'í Month (see chapter 16 for more about this).

How many holy days are there?

There are nine holy days on which Bahá'ís should suspend work. The nineteenth month of the year is devoted to fasting and ends with the beginning of the Bahá'í new year.

Adapting to the New Rhythm

"These, O my Lord, are Thy servants whom no corrupt inclination hath kept back from what Thou didst send down in Thy Book. They have bowed themselves before Thy Cause, and received Thy Book with such resolve as is born of Thee, and observed what Thou hadst prescribed unto them, and chosen to follow that which had been sent down by Thee." Bahá'u'lláh, *Prayers and Meditations*, p. 66.

"O Lord my God! Assist Thy loved ones to be firm in Thy Faith, to walk in Thy ways, to be steadfast in Thy Cause. Give them Thy grace to withstand the onslaught of self and passion, to follow the light of divine guidance." 'Abdu'l-Bahá, *Will and Testament of 'Abdu'l-Bahá,* p. 15.

How do Bahá'ís manage to adapt to this new rhythm of life when surrounded by a very different culture?

". . . the House of Justice advises the Bahá'ís to maintain a balance between their adherence to the Cause and obedience to its laws on the one hand, and their role in society on the other. When an individual becomes a Bahá'í he acquires, as you are aware, a wider loyalty to the Manifestations of God. Having found this new way of life, he should be careful not to isolate himself from his family and his people, and he should show respect for his former religion. The Bahá'ís should, of course, avoid performing any acts which could be considered as implying their membership in another religion or which are contrary to Bahá'í Principles. There is a clear distinction between participating in festive and cultural events, as opposed to performing religious ceremonies and rituals." Letter written on behalf of the Universal House of Justice, in *Lights of Guidance,* no. 465.

How do Bahá'ís make decisions about whether or not to participate in cultural and religious activities of other faiths?

Bahá'ís face the challenge of guarding themselves against two extremes. On the one hand, they do not want to disassociate themselves needlessly from cultural observances and thus alienate themselves from their non-Bahá'í families and friends. On the other hand, they do not wish to continue following abrogated observances of previous dispensations and thus undermine the independence of the Bahá'í Faith. Nor do they want to create undesirable divisions between themselves and their fellow-Bahá'ís all around the world. With this in mind, there is a difference between what Bahá'ís do with other

Bahá'ís and how they share companionship with their non-Bahá'í friends and relations.

A letter written on behalf of the Guardian gives the following guidance as regards Christian holidays, but the general thrust is applicable to Bahá'ís living in other cultures as well:

"As regards the celebration of the Christian Holidays by the believers, it is surely preferable and even highly advisable that the Friends should in their relation to each other discontinue observing such holidays as Christmas and New Year, and to have their festival gatherings of this nature instead during the intercalary days and Naw-Rúz." Letter written on behalf of the Guardian, in *Lights of Guidance,* no. 1029.

How will giving up certain traditions affect the diversity of the world's cultures?

"Giving up such practices does not mean that any people must abandon every other feature of its cultural heritage. On the contrary, what Bahá'u'lláh has done for us all is to provide a standard by which to determine what is pleasing in God's sight, thereby freeing us to maintain those elements of diversity which are unique to our different cultures." The Universal House of Justice, "Traditional Practices in Africa," a letter to an individual believer, dated Dec 16, 1998.

Holy Days on which Work Should Be Suspended

"In the sacred laws of God, in every cycle and dispensation, there are blessed feasts, holidays and workless days. . . . All must enjoy a good time, gather together, hold general meetings, become as one assembly. . . . As it is a blessed day it should not be neglected, nor deprived of results by making it a day devoted to the pursuit of mere pleasure. . . . During such days institutions should be founded that may be of permanent benefit and value to the people." 'Abdu'l-Bahá, in *Lights of Guidance,* no. 1030.

When does a holy day begin?

". . . the Bahá'í day begins and ends at sunset. The night preceding a Holy day is therefore included in the day, and consequently work during that period is forbidden." Shoghi Effendi, *Dawn of a New Day,* p. 68.

Are there exceptions from suspending work on a holy day?

". . . according to our Bahá'í laws, work is forbidden on our Nine Holy Days. Believers who have independent businesses or shops should refrain from working on these days. Those who are in government employ should, on religious grounds, make an effort to be excused from work; all believers, whoever their employers, should do likewise. If the government, or other employers, refuse to grant them these days off, they are not required to forfeit their employment, but they should make every effort to have the independent status of their Faith recognized and their right to hold their own religious Holy Days acknowledged." Letter written on behalf of Shoghi Effendi to the American National Spiritual Assembly, dated July 7, 1947.

Should children stay out of school?

". . . steps should be taken to have Bahá'í children excused, on religious grounds, from attending school on Bahá'í Holy Days wherever possible." Letter written on behalf of the Universal House of Justice to a National Spiritual Assembly, dated October 25, 1947.

Naw-Rúz

Naw-Rúz is the first day of the Bahá'í new year, and Bahá'u'lláh designated it to align with the spring equinox in the Northern Hemisphere. The equinox varies by a day or two in different locations, and the Universal House of Justice decided to let the date vary in tandem with the exact time of the spring equinox in Tehran (the birthplace of Bahá'u'lláh). This means that Naw-Rúz falls on either March 20 or 21. Because the rest of the calendar is affected by the date of Naw-Rúz, the Nineteen-Day-Feasts and most Holy Days vary accordingly.

The Festival of Riḍván (late April and early May)

The word *Riḍván* means *paradise*. For twelve days in the spring, Bahá'ís celebrate the period in 1863 when Bahá'u'lláh camped in a garden near Baghdad, now known as the *Garden of Riḍván*. During this period Bahá'u'lláh proclaimed His mission as God's Messenger for this age. Three of the days—the first, ninth, and twelfth—have been designated as holy days on which work should be suspended.

Declaration of the Báb (May 23 or 24)

It was early in the evening when the Báb declared His mission and so the annual commemoration of this Declaration is held at two hours past sunset.

The Ascension of Bahá'u'lláh (May 28 or 29)

Bahá'u'lláh passed away in the early morning hours, and Shoghi Effendi advised that the observance of His passing be held at 3 a.m.

Martyrdom of the Báb (July 9 or 10)

A noon observance honors the July day in 1850 when the Báb and a young follower of the Bábí Faith were brought before a firing squad in the barracks square of Tabriz. When the smoke emitted by the guns finally cleared, the Báb was nowhere to be seen. When He was found, He was finishing a conversation with His secretary that had been interrupted prior to the scheduled execution.

The commander of the Armenian regiment, Sám Khán, refused to fire a second time and another regiment had to be located. This time the Báb and His companion were killed. Their remains were hidden by the Bábís until 1899, when they were transferred to Palestine. In 1909, 'Abdu'l-Bahá interred the remains in the sepulcher on Mount Carmel now known as the Shrine of the Báb.

The Births of the Báb and Bahá'u'lláh

According to the Islamic lunar calendar, the Births of the Báb and Bahá'u'lláh occurred on consecutive days (the 1st and 2nd of Muharram). In 2014 the Universal House of Justice set the time for these two special celebrations as the first two days of the eighth lunar month after Naw-Rúz. The dates may be as early as

October 20–21 or as late as November 11–12. They are often called the Twin Holy Birthdays.

Two Special Days on which Work is Not Suspended

The Day of the Covenant (November 25 or 26)

When 'Abdu'l-Bahá asked Bahá'ís not to celebrate His birthday because it fell on the same day the Báb declared His mission as a Messenger of God, the Bahá'ís asked Him to suggest something else. He designated a day in late November as the time to remember His appointment as the Center of the Covenant.

Ascension of 'Abdu'l-Bahá (November 27 or 28)

This is observed at 1 a.m., which is the hour of His passing.

The Festival of Ayyám-i-Há

Ayyám-i-Há is a period of several days between the eighteenth and nineteenth months. It is designated as a time for parties, gift-giving, and charitable activities. During this period, Bahá'í are enjoined to "provide good cheer for themselves, their kindred and, beyond them, the poor and needy, and with joy and exultation to hail and glorify their Lord, to sing His praise and magnify His Name." This leaves ample room for cultural diversity and the resulting celebrations are quite different from country to country. Bahá'u'lláh, Kitáb-i-Aqdas, ¶16.

What does Ayyám-i-Há mean?

Ayyám-i-Há means *Days of Há*, or, if fully translated, *five days*. In Arabic *Há* is the letter *H* and has a numerical value of five. Five is a reference to the potential number of days of celebration—there are five days of Ayyám-i-Há in a leap year, but four in a normal year. The letter Há has also been given several spiritual meanings in the holy writings, among which is as a symbol of the essence of God. Some people refer to Ayyám-i-Há as the *Intercalary Days* to indicate that they are not part of the ordinary monthly calendar.

Other Events Sometimes Celebrated By Bahá'í Communities

World Religion Day

This was initiated in 1950 by the National Spiritual Assembly of the United States and is held on the third Sunday in January. The Universal House of Justice describes the underlying concept of this day as "a celebration of the need for and the coming of a world religion for mankind, the Bahá'í Faith. . . ." The Universal House of Justice, in *Lights of Guidance,* no. 1710.

Race Unity Day

In 1957, the National Spiritual Assembly of the United States inaugurated Race Unity Day to promote racial harmony and understanding. It is observed on the second Sunday in June.

Additional Days of Note

United Nations observances like the UN International Day of Peace, International Women's Day, World Food Day, Human Rights Day, and UNICEF Day are supported by some Bahá'í communities.

SPECIAL DAYS IN THE BAHÁ'Í CALENDAR

Suspend work?	Name of Holy Day	Date
yes	Naw-Rúz (New Year's Day)	March 20 or 21
	Riḍván Festival	April 20 or 21–May 1 or 2
yes	First day of Riḍván	April 20 or 21
yes	Ninth Day of Riḍván	April 28 or 29
yes	Twelfth Day of Riḍván	May 1 or 2
yes	Declaration of the Báb	May 23 or 24
yes	Ascension of Bahá'u'lláh	May 28 or 29
yes	Martyrdom of the Báb	July 9 or 10
yes	Birth of the Báb and the Birth of Bahá'u'lláh	These Twin Holy Days vary with the lunar calendar from October 1 to November 12
	Day of the Covenant	November 25 or 26
	Ascension of 'Abdu'l-Bahá	November 27 or 28
	Ayyám-i-Há	Floats between February 25 and March 1
	the Fast	March 1 or 2–19 or 20

ARABIC ENGLISH TRANSLATION FIRST DAY OF THE MONTH

Arabic	English Translation	Dates
Bahá	Splendor	March 20 or 21
Jalál	Glory	April 8 or 9
Jamál	Beauty	April 27 or 28
'Aẓamat	Grandeur	May 16 or 17
Núr	Light	June 4 or 5
Raḥmat	Mercy	June 23 or 24
Kalimát	Words	July 12 or 13
Kamál	Perfection	July 31 or August 1
Asmá'	Names	August 19 or 20
'Izzat	Might	September 7 or 8
Mashíyyat	Will	September 26 or 27
'Ilm	Knowledge	October 15 or 16
Qudrat	Power	November 3 or 4
Qawl	Speech	November 22 or 23
Masá'il	Questions	December 11 or 12
Sharaf	Honor	December 30 or 31
Sulṭán	Sovereignty	January 18 or 19
Mulk	Dominion	February 6 or 7
Ayyám-i-Há	Intercalary Days	Days float between February 25 and March 1
'Alá'	Loftiness	Month of Fasting, begins after Ayyám-i-Há

DAYS OF THE WEEK

Kamál	Perfection	Monday
Fiḍál	Grace	Tuesday
'Idál	Justice	Wednesday
Istijlál	Majesty	Thursday
Istiqlál	Independence	Friday
Jalál	Glory	Saturday
Jamál	Beauty	Sunday

CHAPTER 16

Feasts, Fasting, and Funds

A New Rhythm of Worship

Nineteen-day Feast is the name given to the Bahá'í gathering held once every nineteen days—at the start of each Bahá'í month. It consists of three parts:

- spiritual devotions and readings
- consultation on the affairs of the community
- a social period with refreshments

How did the practice of holding Feast begin?

The Báb began the practice of holding a community gathering for worship once every nineteen days. Bahá'u'lláh affirmed and continued it.

What should happen at a Feast?

During the devotional portion of the program, selections from the Bahá'í writings are read, chanted, or sung. Selections from the scriptures of other religions may also be included. The consultative portion allows time for a general discussion so that each member can have a voice in community affairs, and there are usually reports about what is going on in the Bahá'í community, locally, nationally, and internationally. The social fellowship of the third portion of the Feast includes refreshments, which can range from a simple glass of water or a couple of cookies to an entire meal.

"Let the beloved of God gather together and associate most lovingly and spiritually and happily with one another, conducting themselves with the greatest courtesy and self-restraint.... The host, with complete self-effacement, showing kindness to all, must be a comfort to each one, and serve the friends with his own hands." 'Abdu'l-Bahá, in *The Nineteen Day Feast,* p. 1.

What effect should Feast have on those who attend?

"Assuredly great results will be the outcome of such meetings. Material and spiritual benefits will be assured. All who are present will be intoxicated with the breezes of the Love of God, and the Breath of the Holy Spirit will with tremendous power inspire the hearts. . . . May your hearts be enlightened! May your faces become radiant! May your spirits become illumined! May your thoughts find wider range of vision! May your spiritual susceptibilities be increased! May the realm of God surround you, and may your hearts become the treasury of heaven!" 'Abdu'l-Bahá, in *The Nineteen Day Feast,* pp. 8–9.

What is the global significance of the Nineteen-Day Feast?

"The World Order of Bahá'u'lláh encompasses all units of human society; integrates the spiri-

tual, administrative and social processes of life; and canalizes human expression in its varied forms towards the construction of a new civilization. The Nineteen Day Feast embraces all these aspects at the very base of society. Functioning in the village, the town, the city, it is an institution of which all the people of Bahá are members. It is intended to promote unity, ensure progress, and foster joy.

. . . The Feast may well be seen in its unique combination of modes as the culmination of a great historic process in which primary elements of community life—acts of worship, of festivity and other forms of togetherness— over vast stretches of time have achieved a glorious convergence. The Nineteen Day Feast represents the new stage in this enlightened age to which the basic expression of community life has evolved. Shoghi Effendi has described it as the foundation of the new World Order . . . 'a vital medium for maintaining close and continued contact between the believers themselves and also between them and the body of their elected representatives in the local community.'

[The second portion of the Feast] links the individual to the collective processes by which a society is built or restored . . . the Feast is an arena of democracy at the very root of society." The Universal House of Justice, a letter written to the Followers of Bahá'u'lláh, dated August 27, 1989.

How do diverse cultures influence the Feast?

There is a great deal of lee-way for diversity in the various stages of the Nineteen-Day Feast, including music during the devotional portion, the focus and methods of consultation in the administrative portion, and the manner of showing hospitality during the social portion. As one travels from country to country, it is easy to see both the planetary unity of Feast—everyone observes the same three portions—and the intriguing diversity caused by cultural differences.

What other kinds of gatherings do Bahá'ís hold?

Most Bahá'í communities offer courses about the Bahá'í Faith, referred to as study circles. These courses are a good way to begin to learn about the Bahá'í Faith and, because each course also includes a service component, are a great way to acquire skills that can be used to serve the needs of neighborhoods and communities. There are also classes for children and youth as well as devotional gatherings, holy day obser-vances, regional summer and winter schools, and whatever other groups or programs or parties or occasions a particular community decides to create.

A Month for Fasting

". . . the Fast, which Thou has made a light unto the people of Thy kingdom, even as Thou didst make obligatory prayer a ladder of as-cent unto those who acknowledge Thy unity." Bahá'u'lláh, in *Bahá'í Prayers,* p. 286.

During the final month of the year, 'Alá (Loftiness), Bahá'ís between the ages of fifteen and seventy are asked to fast. There are exemp-tions based on physical infirmities, pregnancy, and other conditions, but everyone else is ex-pected to abstain from food and drink (and smoking) from sunrise to sunset. This means that Bahá'ís rise before dawn to eat breakfast and then wait until after sunset to eat again.

Although Bahá'ís are permitted to fast at other times of the year, Bahá'u'lláh does not encourage it, asking instead that one's energy be directed toward tasks that will profit mankind.

What about Bahá'ís living in extremely high latitudes?

If the hours of daylight are extraordinarily long in a northern country, its National Spiritual Assembly is responsible for determining the appropriate hours of fasting.

What is the good of fasting?

"Fasting is the cause of awakening man. The heart becomes tender and the spirituality of man increases." 'Abdu'l-Bahá, *Star of the West, vol. 3*, p. 305.

"As regards fasting, it constitutes, together with . . . [prayer], the twin pillars that sustain the revealed law of God. They act as stimulants to the soul, revive and purify it, and thus ensure its steady development." Shoghi Effendi, *Directives from the Guardian,* Fasting—The Ordinance of.

How does Bahá'u'lláh describe the period of fasting?

"These are the days whereon Thou hast bidden all men to observe the fast, that through it they may purify their souls and rid themselves of all attachment to anyone but Thee, and that out of their hearts may ascend that which will be worthy of the court of Thy majesty and may well beseem the seat of the revelation of Thy oneness. Grant, O my Lord, that this fast may become a river of life-giving waters and may yield the virtue wherewith Thou hast endowed it." Bahá'u'lláh, *Prayers and Meditations*, p. 79.

A New Rhythm of Giving

". . . the progress and promotion of the Cause of God depend on material means." Bahá'u'lláh, in *The Compilation of Compilations, vol. I,* no. 1099.

Nothing that existeth in the world of being hath ever been or ever will be worthy of mention. However, if a person be graciously favoured to offer a penny-worth— nay even less—in the path of God, this would in His sight be preferable and superior to all the treasures of the earth. It is for this reason that the one true God—exalted be His glory—hath in all His heavenly Scriptures praised those who observe His precepts and bestow their wealth for His sake.

Bahá'u'lláh, in *Huqúqu'lláh,* no. 1.

Who can give to the Bahá'í funds?

Only Bahá'ís may give to the Bahá'í Fund. Contributions are accepted from both adults and children.

How does contributing help the world?

"Our contributions to the Faith are the surest way of lifting once and for all time the burden of hunger and misery from mankind, for it is only through the System of Bahá'u'lláh—Divine in origin—that the world can be gotten on its feet, and want, fear, hunger, war, etc., be eliminated . . . this will lead to the healing of the nations." Shoghi Effendi, in *Lights of Guidance*, no. 413.

What if a person doesn't have much money?

"All the friends of God . . . should contribute to the extent possible, however modest their offering may be. God doth not burden a soul beyond its capacity. Such contributions must come from all centers and all believers. . . . O Friends of God! Be ye assured that in place of these contributions, your agriculture, your industry, and your commerce will be blessed by manifold increases, with goodly gifts and bestowals. He who cometh with one goodly deed will receive a tenfold reward. There is no doubt that the living Lord will abundantly confirm those who expend their wealth in His path." 'Abdu'l-Bahá, *Bahá'í Prayers,* p. 84.

"Contributing to the Fund is a service that every believer can render, be he poor or wealthy; for this is a spiritual responsibility in which the amount given is not important. It is the degree of the sacrifice of the giver, the love with which he makes his gift, and the unity of all the friends in this service which bring spiritual confirmations." The Universal House of Justice, *Messages from the Universal House of Justice, 1963–1986,* no. 13.2.

Are contributions confidential?

Yes. For purposes of bookkeeping and tax records, Spiritual Assemblies must keep a record of the name of contributors, but these names are neither published nor announced.

Can individuals be solicited for contributions?

No. Assemblies may make general appeals to the community for funds and Bahá'ís may discuss the need for funding certain projects, but it is forbidden to solicit funds directly from any individual.

Are contributions tax-deductible in the United States?

Yes. The United States Internal Revenue Service says contributions to the Bahá'í Faith are tax-deductible. Each individual is responsible for keeping a record of his contributions and should also ask the treasurer for receipts to put with his tax records.

How are contributions given?

Local contributions are given to the treasurer of that community. Contributions to other funds—regional, national, and international—can be made online, by mail, or through earmarked funds given to the local treasurer to be forwarded.

How is the money used?

"The members of the Spiritual Assembly will at their own discretion expend it to promote the teaching Campaign, to help the needy, to establish educational Bahá'í institutions, to extend in every way possible their sphere of service. I cherish the hope that all the friends, realizing the necessity of this measure will bestir themselves and contribute, however modestly at first . . ." Shoghi Effendi, *Bahá'í Administration*, p. 42.

An example: During the course of one year in a Bahá'í Community in South Carolina, funds contributed by local Bahá'ís were used in these ways: Monthly sums were sent to the National Bahá'í Fund, the Louis Gregory Museum, the Regional Bahá'í Council for the Southeastern States, and Radio Bahá'í. Bills associated with the upkeep of the Greenville Bahá'í Center were paid and scholarships were provided for several youth who were traveling to a Bahá'í summer school.

Huqúqu'lláh: the Right of God

Huqúqu'lláh is a private spiritual obligation instituted by Bahá'u'lláh. It consists of paying nineteen percent of the increase in one's total assets after allowing for necessary expenses. One's residence, including the money needed to keep a household going, is not included in the sum. Expenses involved in running a business are also considered necessary expenses. Each person is responsible for calculating how much he owes, and it is a wonderful way to separate one's needs from one's wants. Most people calculate it once or twice a year, but some people do it more often as part of tracking monthly income and outgo.

Why is it called the "Right of God?"

In the Bahá'í Dispensation, it is considered that this portion of one's money belongs to God, not to the individual.

Where is the money sent?

Throughout the world there are appointed Trustees of Huqúqu'lláh who accept payments and forward them to the Universal House of Justice. In the United States, payments can be made online, by check, or by money order, and they are tax-deductible. Regional Huqúqu'lláh representatives are available to answer questions and provide information on how to calculate the sum. In the United States, every issue of the American Bahá'í magazine has articles devoted to the subject.

What if a person doesn't have anything in excess of necessary expenses?

Huqúqu'lláh is owed only when a person accumulates money or possessions in excess of what is necessary.

What is the money used for?

It is spent at the discretion of the Universal House of Justice to advance the work of the Bahá'í community, as well as being used for various philanthropic purposes. As Bahá'ís grow in number and the amount of Huqúqu'lláh rises, the amount dedicated to socioeconomic projects will increase.

What are the spiritual benefits of paying Huqúqu'lláh?

"Take heed, O people, lest ye deprive yourselves of this great bounty. We have prescribed this law unto you while We are wholly independent of you and of all that are in the heavens and on the earth. Indeed there lie concealed in this command, mysteries and benefits which are beyond the comprehension of anyone save God, the All-Knowing, the All-Informed. Say, through this injunction God desireth to purify your possessions and enable you to draw nigh unto such stations as none can attain, except those whom God may please." Bahá'u'lláh, in *Huqúqu'lláh,* no. 10.

"O God, my God! Illumine the brows of Thy true lovers, and support them with angelic hosts of certain triumph. Set firm their feet on Thy straight path, and out of Thine ancient bounty open before them the portals of Thy blessings; for they are expending on Thy pathway what Thou hast bestowed upon them, safeguarding Thy Faith, putting their trust in their remembrance of Thee, offering up their hearts for love of Thee, and withholding not what they possess in adoration for Thy Beauty and in their search for ways to please Thee.

O my Lord! Ordain for them a plenteous share, a destined recompense and sure reward.

Verily, Thou art the Sustainer, the Helper, the Generous, the Bountiful, the Ever-Bestowing." 'Abdu'l-Bahá, in *Bahá'í Prayers,* pp. 84–85.

CHAPTER 17

Unity in Diversity

> Ye are all the leaves of one tree and the drops of one ocean.
> Bahá'u'lláh, *Tablets of Bahá'u'lláh*, p. 27.

"O CHILDREN OF MEN! Know ye not why We created you all from the same dust? That no one should exalt himself over the other. Ponder at all times in your hearts how ye were created. Since We have created you all from one same substance it is incumbent on you to be even as one soul, to walk with the same feet, eat with the same mouth and dwell in the same land, that from your inmost being, by your deeds and actions, the signs of oneness and the essence of detachment may be made manifest. Such is My counsel to you, O concourse of light! Heed ye this counsel that ye may obtain the fruit of holiness from the tree of wondrous glory." Bahá'u'lláh, Hidden Words, Arabic, no. 68.

What is the Bahá'í concept of unity?

"O ye that dwell on earth! The distinguishing feature that marketh the preeminent character of this Supreme Revelation consisteth in that We have, on the one hand, blotted out from the pages of God's holy Book whatsoever hath been the cause of strife, of malice and mischief amongst the children of men, and have, on the other, laid down the essential prerequisites of concord, of understanding, of complete and enduring unity." Bahá'u'lláh, *Gleanings from the Writings of Bahá'u'lláh,* no. 43.10.

"O ye loved ones of the Lord! This is the hour when ye must associate with all the earth's peoples in extreme kindliness and love, and be to them the signs and tokens of God's great mercy. Ye must become the very soul of the world, the living spirit in the body of the children of men. In this wondrous Age, at this time when the Ancient Beauty, the Most Great Name, bearing unnumbered gifts, hath risen above the horizon of the world, the Word of God hath infused such awesome power into the inmost essence of humankind that He hath stripped men's human qualities of all effect, and hath, with His all-conquering might, unified the peoples in a vast sea of oneness." 'Abdu'l-Bahá, *Selections from the Writings of 'Abdu'l-Bahá,* no. 7.2.

"Whatever is conducive to the unity of the world of mankind is most acceptable and praiseworthy; whatever is the cause of discord and disunion is saddening and deplorable." 'Abdu'l-Bahá, *The Promulgation of Universal Peace,* p. 76.

Will unity bring peace?

"When Bahá'u'lláh proclaimed His Message to the world in the nineteenth century He made it abundantly clear that the first step essential for the peace and progress of mankind was its unification. As He says, 'The well-being of mankind, its peace and security are unattainable unless and until its unity is firmly established.' To this day, however, you will find most people take the opposite point of view: they look upon unity as an ultimate, almost unattainable goal and concentrate first on remedying all the other ills of mankind. If they did but know it, these other ills are but various symptoms and side effects of the basic disease—disunity." The Universal House of Justice, *Messages from the Universal House of Justice, 1963–1986,* no. 55.3.

"World order can be founded only on an unshakable consciousness of the oneness of mankind, a spiritual truth which all the human sciences confirm. Anthropology, physiology, psychology, recognize only one human species, albeit infinitely varied in the secondary aspects of life. Recognition of this truth requires abandonment of prejudice—prejudice of every kind—race, class, color, creed, nation, sex, degree of material civilization, everything which enables people to consider themselves superior to others." The Universal House of Justice, in *The Compilation of Compilations, vol. II,* no. 2122.

What are the consequences of disunity?

"Every edifice is made of many different stones, yet each depends on the other to such an extent that if one were displaced the whole building would suffer; if one is faulty the structure is imperfect." 'Abdu'l-Bahá, *Paris Talks,* no. 15.11.

"How pathetic indeed are the efforts of those leaders of human institutions who, in utter disregard of the spirit of the age, are striving to adjust national processes, suited to the ancient days of self-contained nations, to an age which must either achieve the unity of the world, as adumbrated by Bahá'u'lláh, or perish." Shoghi Effendi, *The World Order of Bahá'u'lláh,* p. 36.

"The whole of mankind is groaning, is dying to be led to unity, and to terminate its age-long martyrdom. And yet it stubbornly refuses to embrace the light and acknowledge the sovereign authority of the one Power that can extricate it from its entanglements, and avert the woeful calamity that threatens to engulf it." Shoghi Effendi, *The World Order of Bahá'u'lláh,* p. 201.

"Disunity is a danger that the nations and peoples of the earth can no longer endure; the consequences are too terrible to contemplate, too obvious to require any demonstration." The Universal House of Justice, *Messages from the Universal House of Justice, 1963–1986,* no. 438.54.

Race Unity

What are the effects of racism?

"Racism, one of the most baneful and persistent evils, is a major barrier to peace. Its practice perpetrates too outrageous a violation of the dignity of human beings to be countenanced under any pretext. Racism retards the unfoldment of the boundless potentialities of its victims, corrupts its perpetrators, and blights human progress. Recognition of the oneness of mankind, implemented by appropriate legal measures, must be universally upheld if this problem is to be overcome." The Universal

House of Justice, *Messages from the Universal House of Justice, 1963–1986,* no. 438.29.

Why do we have different skin colors?

"Because of the climatic differences of the zones, through the passing of ages colors have become different. In the torrid zone, on account of the intensity of the effect of the sun throughout the ages the black race appeared. In the frigid zone, on account of the severity of the cold and the ineffectiveness of the heat of the sun throughout the ages the white race appeared. In the temperate zone, the yellow, brown and red races came into existence. But in reality mankind is one race. Because it is of one race unquestionably there must be unity and harmony and no separation or discord." 'Abdu'l-Bahá, cited in a letter written on behalf of the Universal House of Justice, *The Power of Unity,* p. 48.

What is the best skin color?

"There are no whites and blacks before God. All colors are one, and that is the color of servitude to God. Scent and color are not important. If the heart is pure, white or black or any color makes no difference. God does not look at colors; He looks at the hearts. He whose heart is pure is better. He whose character is better is more pleasing." 'Abdu'l-Bahá, *The Promulgation of Universal Peace,* p. 60.

"If you beheld a garden in which all the plants were the same as to form, color and perfume, it would not seem beautiful to you at all, but, rather, monotonous and dull. The garden which is pleasing to the eye and which makes the heart glad, is the garden in which are growing side by side flowers of every hue, form and perfume, and the joyous contrast of color is what makes for charm and beauty. So is it with trees. An orchard full of fruit trees is a delight; so is a plantation planted with many species of shrubs. It is just the diversity and variety that constitutes its charm; each flower, each tree, each fruit, beside being beautiful in itself, brings out by contrast the qualities of the others, and shows to advantage the special loveliness of each and all." 'Abdu'l-Bahá, *Paris Talks,* no. 15.6.

How can racism be overcome?

"Illumine and hallow your hearts; let them not be profaned by the thorns of hate or the thistles of malice. Ye dwell in one world, and have been created through the operation of one Will. Blessed is he who mingleth with all men in a spirit of utmost kindliness and love." Bahá'u'lláh, *Gleanings from the Writings of Bahá'u'lláh,* no. 156.1.

"Shut your eyes to estrangement, then fix your gaze upon unity. Cleave tenaciously unto that which will lead to the well-being and tranquillity of all mankind. This span of earth is but one homeland and one habitation." Bahá'u'lláh, *Tablets of Bahá'u'lláh,* p. 67.

How should I relate to those with a different skin color?

"The diversity in the human family should be the cause of love and harmony, as it is in music where many different notes blend together in the making of a perfect chord. If you meet those of different race and color from yourself, do not mistrust them and withdraw yourself into your shell of conventionality, but rather be glad and show them kindness. Think of them as different colored roses growing in the beautiful garden of humanity and rejoice to be among them." 'Abdu'l-Bahá, *Paris Talks,* no. 15.7.

Will marriage between different races bring unity?

"Thou must endeavor that they intermarry. There is no greater means to bring about affection between the white and the black than the influence of the Word of God. Likewise marriage between these two races will wholly destroy and eradicate the root of enmity." 'Abdu'l-Bahá, cited in a letter written on behalf of the Universal House of Justice, *The Power of Unity,* p. 55.

Is it easy for Americans to overcome racism?

"Let neither [race] think that anything short of genuine love, extreme patience, true humility, consummate tact, sound initiative, mature wisdom, and deliberate, persistent, and prayerful effort, can succeed in blotting out the stain which this patent evil has left on the fair name of their common country (America)." Shoghi Effendi, *The Advent of Divine Justice,* ¶58.

Unity Between the Sexes: the Equality of Women and Men

"Know thou, O handmaid, that in the sight of Bahá, women are accounted the same as men, and God hath created all humankind in His own image, and after His own likeness. That is, men and women alike are the revealers of His names and attributes, and from the spiritual viewpoint there is no difference between them. Whosoever draweth nearer to God, that one is the most favored, whether man or woman. How many a handmaid, ardent and devoted, hath, within the sheltering shade of Bahá, proved superior to the men, and surpassed the famous of the earth." 'Abdu'l-Bahá, *Selections from the Writings of 'Abdu'l-Bahá*, no. 38.3.

"The truth is that all mankind are the creatures and servants of one God, and in His estimate all are human. Man is a generic term applying to all humanity. The biblical statement "let us make man in our image, after our likeness" does not mean that woman was not created. The image and likeness of God apply to her as well. . . .

To accept and observe a distinction which God has not intended in creation is ignorance and superstition." 'Abdu'l-Bahá, *The Promulgation of Universal Peace*, pp. 104–5.

Why has there been inequality?

". . . history furnishes evidence that during the past centuries there have been great women as well as great men; but in general, owing to lack of educational advantages, women have been restricted and deprived of opportunity to become fully qualified and representative of humankind. When given the opportunity for acquiring education, they have shown equal capacity with men. Some philosophers and writers have considered woman naturally and by creation inferior to man, claiming as a proof that the brain of man is larger and heavier than that of woman. This is frail and faulty evidence, inasmuch as small brains are often found coupled with superior intellect and large brains possessed by those who are ignorant, even imbecilic. The truth is that God has endowed all humankind with intelligence and perception and has confirmed all as His servants and children; therefore, in the plan and estimate of God there is no distinction between male or female. The soul that manifests pure deeds and spiritual graces is most precious in His sight and nearer to Him in its attainments." 'Abdu'l-Bahá, *The Promulgation of Universal Peace*, pp. 394–95.

Does equality of women and men mean sameness?

"Equality between men and women does not, indeed physiologically it cannot, mean identity of functions. In some things women excel men, for other men are better fitted than women, while in very many things the difference of sex is of no effect at all. The differences of function are most apparent in family life. The capacity for motherhood has many far-reaching implications which are recognized in Bahá'í Law. For example, when it is not possible to educate all one's children, daughters receive preference over sons as mothers are the first educators of the next generation. Again, for physiological reasons, women are granted certain exemptions from fasting that are not applicable to men." The Universal House of Justice, *Messages from*

the Universal House of Justice, 1963–1986, no. 166.2.

Will men benefit from equality?

"The world of humanity is possessed of two wings: the male and the female. So long as these two wings are not equivalent in strength, the bird will not fly. Until womankind reaches the same degree as man, until she enjoys the same arena of activity, extraordinary attainment for humanity will not be realized; humanity cannot wing its way to heights of real attainment. When the two wings . . . become equivalent in strength, enjoying the same prerogatives, the flight of man will be exceedingly lofty and extraordinary. Therefore, woman must receive the same education as man and all inequality be adjusted. Then, imbued with the same virtues as man, rising through all the degrees of human attainment, women will become the peers of men, and until this equality is established, true progress and attainment for the human race will not be facilitated." 'Abdu'l-Bahá, *The Promulgation of Universal Peace,* p. 529.

"Again, it is well established in history that where woman has not participated in human affairs the outcomes have never attained a state of completion and perfection. On the other hand, every influential undertaking of the human world wherein woman has been a participant has attained importance. This is historically true and beyond disproof even in religion. Jesus Christ had twelve disciples and among His followers a woman known as Mary Magdalene. Judas Iscariot had become a traitor and hypocrite, and after the crucifixion the remaining eleven disciples were wavering and undecided. It is certain from the evidence of the Gospels that the one who comforted them and reestablished their faith was Mary Magdalene." 'Abdu'l-Bahá, *The Promulgation of Universal Peace,* p. 185.

"And let it be known once more that until woman and man recognize and realize equality, social and political progress here or anywhere will not be possible. For the world of humanity consists of two parts or members; one is woman; the other is man. Until these two members are equal in strength, the oneness of humanity cannot be established, and the happiness and felicity of mankind will not be a reality." 'Abdu'l-Bahá, *The Promulgation of Universal Peace,* pp. 105–6.

How will the equality of women and men bring peace?

"When all mankind shall receive the same opportunity of education and the equality of men and women be realized, the foundations of war will be utterly destroyed. Without equality this will be impossible because all differences and distinction are conducive to discord and strife. Equality between men and women is conducive to the abolition of warfare for the reason that women will never be willing to sanction it." 'Abdu'l-Bahá, *The Promulgation of Universal Peace,* p. 243.

"Consider a son reared and trained twenty years by a devoted mother . . . how agonizing then to sacrifice him upon the battlefield! Therefore, the mothers will not sanction war nor be satisfied with it. So it will come to pass that when women participate fully and equally in the affairs of the world, when they enter confidently and capably the great arena of laws and politics, war will cease; for women will be the obstacle and hindrance to it. This is true and without doubt." 'Abdu'l-Bahá, *The Promulgation of Universal Peace,* p. 186.

What will the world be like when men and women achieve equality?

"The world in the past has been ruled by force, and man has dominated over woman by reason of his more forceful and aggressive qualities both of the body and mind. But the balance is already shifting; force is losing its weight and mental alertness, intuition, and the spiritual qualities of love and service, in which woman is strong, are gaining ascendancy. Hence the new age will be an age less masculine and more permeated with the feminine ideals, or, to speak more exactly, will be an age in which the masculine and feminine elements of civilization will be more evenly balanced." 'Abdu'l-Bahá, cited in Esslemont, *Bahá'u'lláh and the New Era,* p. 164.

Unity in Action

"Your souls are as waves on the sea of the spirit; although each individual is a distinct wave, the ocean is one, all are united in God.

"Every heart should radiate unity, so that the Light of the one Divine Source of all may shine forth bright and luminous. We must not consider the separate waves alone, but the entire sea. We should rise from the individual to the whole. The spirit is as one great ocean and the waves thereof are the souls of men." 'Abdu'l-Bahá, *Paris Talks,* nos. 28.1–2.

"Consort together in brotherly love, be ready to lay down your lives one for the other, and not only for those who are dear to you, but for all humanity. Look upon the whole human race as members of one family, all children of God; and, in so doing, you will see no difference between them." 'Abdu'l-Bahá, *Paris Talks,* no. 53.11.

How should we look at each other?

"Cleanse ye your eyes, so that ye behold no man as different from yourselves. See ye no strangers; rather see all men as friends, for love and unity come hard when ye fix your gaze on otherness. And in this new and wondrous age, the Holy Writings say that we must be at one with every people; that we must see neither harshness nor injustice, neither malevolence, nor hostility, nor hate, but rather turn our eyes toward the heaven of ancient glory. For each of the creatures is a sign of God, and it was by the grace of the Lord and His power that each did step into the world; therefore they are not strangers, but in the family; not aliens, but friends, and to be treated as such." 'Abdu'l-Bahá, *Selections from the Writings of 'Abdu'l-Bahá,* no. 8.7.

How can we learn to appreciate differences?

"As difference in degree of capacity exists among human souls, as difference in capability is found, therefore, individualities will differ one from another. But in reality this is a reason for unity and not for discord and enmity. If the flowers of a garden were all of one color, the effect would be monotonous to the eye; but if the colors are variegated, it is most pleasing and wonderful. The difference in adornment of color and capacity of reflection among the flowers gives the garden its beauty and charm. Therefore, although we are of different individualities, different in ideas and of various fragrances, let us strive like flowers of the same divine garden to live together in harmony. Even though each soul has its own individual perfume and color, all are reflecting the same light, all contributing fragrance to the same breeze which blows through the garden, all continuing to grow in complete harmony and accord." 'Abdu'l-Bahá, *The Promulgation of Universal Peace,* p. 33.

What if I meet someone I don't like?

"Wherefore must the loved ones of God associate in affectionate fellowship with stranger and friend alike, showing forth to all the utmost loving-kindness, disregarding the degree of their capacity, never asking whether they deserve to be loved. In every instance let the friends be considerate and infinitely kind. Let them never be defeated by the malice of the people, by their aggression and their hate, no matter how intense. If others hurl their darts against you, offer them milk and honey in return; if they poison your lives, sweeten their souls; if they injure you, teach them how to be comforted; if they inflict a wound upon you, be a balm to their sores; if they sting you hold to their lips a refreshing cup." 'Abdu'l-Bahá, *Selections from the Writings of 'Abdu'l-Bahá,* no. 8.8.

Can I really be a friend to everyone?

"One must see in every human being only that which is worthy of praise. When this is done, one can be a friend to the whole human race. If, however, we look at people from the standpoint of their faults, then being a friend to them is a formidable task. 'Abdu'l-Bahá, *Selections from the Writings of 'Abdu'l-Bahá,* no. 144.2.

How should I react when someone's opinion differs from mine?

". . . when you meet those whose opinions differ from your own, do not turn away your face from them. All are seeking truth, and there are many roads leading thereto. Truth has many aspects, but it remains always and forever one.

Do not allow difference of opinion, or diversity of thought to separate you from your fellowmen, or to be the cause of dispute, hatred and strife in your hearts.

Rather, search diligently for the truth and make all men your friends. . . .

Leave all thought of self, and strive only to be obedient and submissive to the Will of God. In this way only shall we become citizens of the Kingdom of God and attain unto life everlasting." 'Abdu'l-Bahá, *Paris Talks,* nos. 15.8–12.

How is it possible to put aside personal differences?

"If any differences arise amongst you, behold Me standing before your face, and overlook the faults of one another for My name's sake and as a token of your love for My manifest and resplendent Cause." Bahá'u'lláh, *Gleanings from the Writings of Bahá'u'lláh,* no. 146.1.

"Love the creatures for the sake of God and not for themselves. You will never become angry or impatient if you love them for the sake of God. Humanity is not perfect. There are imperfections in every human being, and you will always become unhappy if you look toward the people themselves. But if you look toward God, you will love them and be kind to them, for the world of God is the world of perfection and complete mercy. Therefore, do not look at the shortcomings of anybody; see with the sight of forgiveness. The imperfect eye beholds imperfections. The eye that covers faults looks toward the Creator of souls. He created them, trains and provides for them, endows them with capacity and life, sight and hearing; therefore, they are the signs of His grandeur." 'Abdu'l-Bahá, *The Promulgation of Universal Peace,* p. 128.

Is it important to refrain from backbiting and gossip?

"Breathe not the sins of others so long as thou art thyself a sinner." Bahá'u'lláh, Hidden Words, Arabic, no. 27.

"He must never seek to exalt himself above anyone, must wash away from the tablet of his heart every trace of pride and vainglory, must cling unto patience and resignation, observe silence and refrain from idle talk. For the tongue is a smoldering fire, and excess of speech a deadly poison. Material fire consumeth the body, whereas the fire of the tongue devoureth both heart and soul. The force of the former lasteth but for a time, whilst the effects of the latter endureth a century." Bahá'u'lláh, *Gleanings from the Writings of Bahá'u'lláh,* no. 125.2.

. . . regard backbiting as a grievous error . . . inasmuch as backbiting quencheth the light of the heart, and extinguisheth the life of the soul.

Bahá'u'lláh, *Gleanings from the Writings of Bahá'u'lláh,* no. 125.3.

"O companion of My throne! Hear no evil, and see no evil, abase not thyself, neither sigh and weep. Speak no evil, that thou mayest not hear it spoken unto thee, and magnify not the faults of others that thine own faults may not appear great; and wish not the abasement of anyone, that thine own abasement be not exposed. Live then the days of thy life, that are less than a fleeting moment, with thy mind stainless, thy heart unsullied, thy thoughts pure, and thy nature sanctified, so that, free and content, thou mayest put away this mortal frame, and repair unto the mystic paradise and abide in the eternal kingdom for evermore." Bahá'u'lláh, Hidden Words, Persian, no. 44.

Unity Through Consultation

In administrative institutions, as well as in their personal lives and even in their businesses, Bahá'ís use a non-adversarial method of making decisions that is known as consultation. A unique and extremely important feature of Bahá'í consultation is that when an idea is put forth, it immediately becomes the property of the whole group. This shared ownership of ideas helps prevent egotistical and partisan struggles for power while maximizing opportunities for creative thinking and cooperative problem-solving.

"The question of consultation is of the utmost importance, and is one of the most potent instruments conducive to the tranquility and felicity of the people." 'Abdu'l-Bahá, in *The Compilation of Compilations, vol. I,* no. 179.

What kinds of things should be settled through consultation?

"Settle all things, both great and small, by consultation. Without prior consultation, take no important step in your own personal affairs. Concern yourselves with one another. Help along one another's projects and plans. Grieve over one another. Let none in the whole country go in need. Befriend one another until ye become as a single body, one and all . . ." 'Abdu'l-Bahá, in *Lights of Guidance,* no. 588.

How should one participate in consultation?

". . . consultation must have for its object the investigation of truth. He who expresses an opinion should not voice it as correct and right but set it forth as a contribution to the consensus of opinion; for the light of reality becomes apparent when two opinions coincide. . . . Man should weigh his opinions with the utmost serenity, calmness and composure. Before expressing his own views he should carefully consider the views already advanced by others.

If he finds that a previously expressed opinion is more true and worthy, he should accept it immediately and not willfully hold to an opinion of his own." 'Abdu'l-Bahá, *The Promulgation of Universal Peace,* pp. 99–100.

What is the power of consultation?

". . . the views of several individuals are assuredly preferable to one man, even as the power of a number of men is of course greater than the power of one man. Thus consultation is acceptable in the presence of the Almighty, and hath been enjoined upon the believers, so that they may confer upon ordinary and personal matters, as well as on affairs which are general in nature and universal. For instance, when a man hath a project to accomplish, should he consult with some of his brethren, that which is agreeable will of course be investigated and unveiled to his eyes, and the truth will be disclosed. Likewise on a higher level, should the people of a village consult one another about their affairs, the right solution will certainly be revealed. In like manner, the members of each profession, such as in industry, should consult, and those in commerce should similarly consult on business affairs. In short, consultation is desirable and acceptable in all things and on all issues." 'Abdu'l-Bahá, in *Lights of Guidance,* no. 580.

"O Thou kind lord! O Thou Who art generous and merciful! We are the servants of Thy threshold and are gathered beneath the sheltering shadow of Thy divine unity. The sun of Thy mercy is shining upon all, and the clouds of Thy bounty shower upon all. Thy gifts encompass all, Thy loving providence sustains all, Thy protection overshadows all, and the glances of Thy favor are cast upon all. O Lord! Grant Thine infinite bestowals, and let the light of Thy guidance shine. Illumine the eyes, gladden the hearts with abiding joy. Confer a new spirit upon all people and bestow upon them eternal life. Unlock the gates of true understanding and let the light of faith shine resplendent. Gather all people beneath the shadow of Thy bounty and cause them to unite in harmony, so that they may become as the rays of one sun, as the waves of one ocean, and as the fruit of one tree. May they drink from the same fountain. May they be refreshed by the same breeze. May they receive illumination from the same source of light. Thou art the Giver, the Merciful, the Omnipotent." 'Abdu'l-Bahá, *The Promulgation of Universal Peace,* p. 160.

CHAPTER 18

Marriage and Divorce and Sexual Conduct

> God hath prescribed matrimony
> unto you.
>
> Bahá'u'lláh,
> Kitáb-i-Aqdas, ¶63.

"From separation doth every kind of hurt and harm proceed, but the union of created things doth ever yield most laudable results. From the pairing of even the smallest particles in the world of being are the grace and bounty of God made manifest; and the higher the degree, the more momentous is the union. 'Glory be to Him Who hath created all the pairs, of such things as earth produceth, and out of men themselves, and of things beyond their ken.' And above all other unions is that between human beings, especially when it cometh to pass in the love of God. Thus is the primal oneness made to appear;

thus is laid the foundation of love in the spirit." 'Abdu'l-Bahá, *Selections from the Writings of 'Abdu'l-Bahá,* no. 87.2.

What is the purpose of marriage?

"And when He desired to manifest grace and beneficence to men, and to set the world in order, He revealed observances and created laws; among them He established the law of marriage, made it as a fortress for well-being and salvation, and enjoined it upon us in that which was sent down out of the heaven of sanctity in His Most Holy Book. He saith, great is His glory: 'Marry, O people, that from you may appear he who will remember Me amongst My servants; this is one of My commandments unto you; obey it as an assistance to yourselves.'" Bahá'u'lláh, in *Bahá'í Prayers,* p. 118.

". . . Bahá'u'lláh explicitly reveals in His Book of laws that the very purpose of marriage is the procreation of children who, when grown up, will be able to know God and to recognize and observe His Commandments and Laws as revealed through His Messengers. Marriage is thus, according to the Bahá'í Teachings, primarily a social and moral act. It has a purpose which transcends the immediate personal needs and interests of the parties." Shoghi Effendi, in *Lights of Guidance,* no. 1160.

Is the bond of marriage meant to be physical or spiritual?

"Marriage, among the mass of the people, is a physical bond, and this union can only be temporary, since it is foredoomed to a physical separation at the close.

Among the people of Bahá, however, marriage must be a union of the body and of the spirit as well, for here both husband and wife are aglow with the same wine, both are enamored of the same matchless Face, both live and move through the same spirit, both are illumined by the same glory. This connection between them is a spiritual one, hence it is a bond that will abide forever. Likewise do they enjoy strong and lasting ties in the physical world as well, for if the marriage is based both on the spirit and the body, that union is a true one, hence it will endure. If, however, the bond is physical and nothing more, it is sure to be only temporary, and must inexorably end in separation.

When, therefore, the people of Bahá undertake to marry, the union must be a true relationship, a spiritual coming together as well as a physical one, so that throughout every phase of life, and in all the worlds of God, their union will endure; for this real oneness is a gleaming out of the love of God." 'Abdu'l-Bahá, *Selections from the Writings of 'Abdu'l-Bahá,* nos. 84.1–3.

How important is the sexual aspect of marriage?

"Bahá'u'lláh has urged marriage upon all people as the natural and rightful way of life. He has also, however, placed strong emphasis on its spiritual nature, which, while in no way precluding a normal physical way of life, is the most essential aspect of marriage. That two people should live their lives in love and harmony is of far greater importance than that they should be consumed with passion for each other. The one is a great rock of strength on which to lean in time of need; the other is a purely temporary thing which may at any time die out." Shoghi Effendi, in *Lights of Guidance,* no. 1268.

How can one prepare for marriage?

". . . man should know his own self, and recognize that which leadeth unto loftiness or lowliness, glory or abasement." Bahá'u'lláh, *Tablets of Bahá'u'lláh,* p. 35.

"Bahá'í marriage is the commitment of the two parties one to the other, and their mutual attachment of mind and heart. Each must, however, exercise the utmost care to become thoroughly acquainted with the character of the other, that the binding covenant between them may be a tie that will endure forever. Their purpose must be this: to become loving companions and comrades and at one with each other for time and eternity. . . ." 'Abdu'l-Bahá, *Selections from the Writings of 'Abdu'l-Bahá,* no. 86.1.

What does it mean to be at one with each other for eternity?

"What is meant is that marriage should lead to a profound friendship of spirit, which will endure in the next world, where there is no sex, and no giving and taking in marriage; just the way we should establish with our parents, our children, our brothers and sisters and friends a deep spiritual bond which will be everlasting and not merely physical bonds of human relationship." Letter written on behalf of Shoghi Effendi to an individual believer, December 4, 1954.

What does a Bahá'í wedding include?

A Bahá'í wedding ceremony is very simple. In the presence of two witnesses selected by the couple and accepted by the Local Spiritual Assembly, both bride and groom recite this vow: "We will all, verily, abide by the Will of God." The ceremony may also incorporate other readings, music, etc.

Is parental consent necessary for marriage?

"Bahá'u'lláh has clearly stated the consent of all living parents is required for a Bahá'í marriage. . . . This great law He has laid down to strengthen the social fabric, to knit closer the ties of the home, to place a certain gratitude and respect in the hearts of children for those who have given them life and sent their souls out on the eternal journey towards their Creator." Shoghi Effendi, cited in Kitáb-i-Aqdas, note no. 93, p. 207.

What are the responsibilities of the Local Spiritual Assembly in a wedding?

The Assembly should be contacted far enough in advance so that it can review and approve the parental consent and ensure that arrangements for the Bahá'í ceremony are in conformity with Baha'i principles and the requirements of civil law of that particular country. If difficulties arise in obtaining consent, the Assembly will endeavor to help.

Bahá'í marriage ceremonies are legally recognized throughout the United States. The Assembly representative who signs the civil license is often the person who is the current chair or secretary but can be anyone authorized by the Assembly.

Is marriage an obligation?

Marriage is not required and it is left to each individual to decide whether to lead a family life or a celibate life.

Will it ruin someone's life to remain single?

"It should, moreover, be borne in mind that although to be married is highly desirable, and Bahá'u'lláh has strongly recommended it, it is not the central purpose of life. If a person has to wait a considerable period before finding a spouse, or if ultimately, he or she must remain single, it does not mean that he or she is thereby unable to fulfill his or her life's purpose." The Universal House of Justice, *Messages from the Universal House of Justice, 1968–1986,* no. 126.9.

Sexual Conduct

"Enter ye into wedlock, that after you another may arise in your stead. We, verily, have forbidden you lechery, and not that which is conducive to fidelity." Bahá'u'lláh, Epistle to the Son of the Wolf, p. 49.

"The Bahá'í Faith recognizes the value of the sex impulse, but condemns its illegitimate and improper expressions such as free love, companionate marriage and others, all of which it considers positively harmful to man and to the society in which he lives. The proper use of the sex instinct is the natural right of every individual, and it is precisely for this very purpose that the institution of marriage has been established. The Bahá'ís do not believe in the suppression of the sex impulse but in its regulation and control." Shoghi Effendi, in *Lights of Guidance,* no. 1156.

"Bahá'í teachings on sexual morality centre on marriage and the family as the bedrock of the whole structure of human society and are designed to protect and strengthen that divine institution. Thus Bahá'í law restricts permissible sexual intercourse to that between a man and the woman to whom he is married." The Universal House of Justice, in *Lights of Guidance,* no. 225.

The Value of Chastity

God is My witness! The brightness of the light of chastity sheddeth its illumination upon the worlds of the spirit, and its fragrance is wafted even unto the Most Exalted Paradise.

Bahá'u'lláh, cited in Shoghi Effendi,
The Advent of Divine Justice, ¶48.

What does being chaste imply?

"Chastity implies both before and after marriage an unsullied, chaste sex life. Before marriage absolutely chaste, after marriage absolutely faithful to one's chosen companion. Faithful in all sexual acts, faithful in word and in deed." Shoghi Effendi, in *Lights of Guidance,* no. 1212.

Is chastity equally important for men and women?

". . . the Bahá'í conception of sex is based on the belief that chastity should be strictly practiced by both sexes, not only because it is in itself highly commendable ethically, but also due to its being the only way to a happy and successful marital life. Sex relationships of any form, outside marriage, are not permissible therefore, and whoso violates this rule will not only be responsible to God, but will incur the necessary punishment from society." Shoghi Effendi, in *Lights of Guidance,* no. 1157.

How can youth be chaste in current society?

"The Bahá'í youth should study the teachings on chastity and, with these in mind, should avoid any behaviour which would arouse passions which would tempt them to violate them. In deciding what acts are permissible to them in the light of these considerations the youth must use their own judgment, following the guidance of their consciences and the advice of their parents.

"If Bahá'í youth combine such personal purity with an attitude of uncensorious forbearance towards others they will find that those who may have criticized or even mocked them will come, in time, to respect them. They will, moreover, be laying a firm foundation for true married happiness." The Universal House of Justice, in *Lights of Guidance,* no. 1213.

What effect does adultery have on a person's soul?

". . . Bahá'u'lláh says adultery retards the progress of the soul in the afterlife—so grievous is it . . ." Shoghi Effendi, in *Lights of Guidance,* no. 1159.

Is it important to try to obey the laws of sexual conduct?

"Fear ye the Merciful, O peoples of the world. Commit not that which is forbidden you in Our Holy Tablet, and be not of those who rove distractedly in the wilderness of their desires." Bahá'u'lláh, Kitáb-i-Aqdas, ¶107.

What about homosexuality?

Homosexual relations are forbidden, but the Bahá'í Faith calls on all of its followers to behave with tolerance and understanding toward everyone and to refrain from imposing its moral standards on a person who has not accepted the Revelation of Bahá'u'lláh.

"While recognizing the Divine origin and force of the sex impulse in man, religion teaches that it must be controlled, and Bahá'u'lláh's Law confines its expression to the marriage relationship. The unmarried homosexual is therefore in the same position as anyone else who does not marry. The Law of God requires them to practice chastity." The Universal House of Justice, in *Lights of Guidance,* p. 366

"While Bahá'ís hold specific beliefs about human identity, sexuality, personal morality, and individual and social transformation, they also believe that individuals must be free to investigate truth and should not be coerced . . . To regard a person who has a homosexual orientation with prejudice or disdain is entirely against the spirit of the Faith. And where occasion demands, it would be appropriate to speak out or act against unjust or oppressive measures directed towards homosexuals." The Universal

House of Justice, in a letter to an individual dated May 9, 2014.

Are there any Bahá'í teachings on transsexuality?

"The House of Justice has not found any text in the Baha'i writings which deals explicitly with the subjects of transsexuality or surgical operations carried out to change sex or to establish a single sex. It has decided that changes of sex or attempts to change sex should, at the present time, be considered medical questions on which advice and guidance should be sought from experts in that field." Letter to an individual written on behalf of the Universal House of Justice, dated August 32, 1983.

Can struggling to obey the laws of sexual conduct help a person grow spiritually?

"Every believer needs to remember that an essential characteristic of this physical world is that we are constantly faced with trials, tribulations, hardships and sufferings and that by overcoming them we achieve our moral and spiritual development; that we must seek to accomplish in the future what we may have failed to do in the past; that this is the way God tests His servants and we should look upon every failure or shortcoming as an opportunity to try again and to acquire a fuller consciousness of

the Divine Will and purpose." The Universal House of Justice, in *Lights of Guidance,* no. 1226.

Divorce

"God doth verily love union and concord, and abhorreth separation and divorce." Bahá'u'lláh, in *The Compilation of Compilations, vol. I,* no. 521.

"They must strictly refrain from divorce unless something ariseth which compelleth them to separate because of their aversion for each other, in that case with the knowledge of the Spiritual Assembly they may decide to separate. They must then be patient and wait one complete year. If during this year harmony is not re-established between them, then divorce may be realized. It should not happen that upon the occurrence of a slight friction or displeasure between husband and wife, the husband would think of union with some other woman, or God forbid, the wife also think of another husband. This is contrary to the standard of heavenly value and true chastity. The friends of God must so live and conduct themselves, and evince such excellence of character and conduct, as to make others astonished. The love between husband and wife should not be purely physical, nay rather it must be spiritual and heavenly. These two souls should be considered as one soul. How difficult it would be to divide a single soul! Nay, greater would be the difficulty.

In short, the foundation of the Kingdom of God is based upon harmony and love, oneness, relationship and union, not upon differences, especially between husband and wife. If one of these two become the cause of divorce, that one will unquestionably fall into great difficulties, will become the victim of formidable calamities and experience deep remorse." 'Abdu'l-Bahá, in *Lights of Guidance,* no. 1306.

How does divorce affect the rest of the world?

"Regarding the Bahá'í teachings on divorce. While the latter has been made permissible by Bahá'u'lláh yet He has strongly discouraged its practice, for if not checked and seriously controlled it leads gradually to the disruption of family life and to the disintegration of society." Letter written on behalf of Shoghi Effendi, in *The Compilation of Compilations, vol. I,* no. 534.

What is one of the prayers for marriage?

O my Lord, O my Lord! These two bright orbs are wedded in Thy love, conjoined in servitude to Thy Holy Threshold, united in ministering to Thy Cause. Make Thou this marriage to be as threading lights of Thine abounding grace, O my Lord, the All-Merciful, and luminous rays of Thy bestowals, O Thou the Beneficent, the Ever-Giving, that there may branch out from this great tree boughs that will grow green and flourishing through the gifts that rain down from Thy clouds of grace.

Verily Thou art the Generous, verily Thou art the Almighty, verily Thou art the Compassionate, the All-Merciful. 'Abdu'l-Bahá, *Selections from the Writings of 'Abdu'l-Bahá,* nos. 87.3–4.

CHAPTER 19

Family Life and the Education of Children

"Compare the nations of the world to the members of a family. A family is a nation in miniature. Simply enlarge the circle of the household and you have the nation. Enlarge the circle of nations and you have all humanity. The conditions surrounding the family surround the nation. The happenings in the family are the happenings in the life of the nation. Would it add to the progress and advancement of a family if dissensions should arise among its members, fighting, pillaging each other, jealous and revengeful of injury, seeking selfish advantage? Nay, this would be the cause of the effacement of progress and advancement. So it is in the great family of nations, for nations are but an aggregate of families." 'Abdu'l-Bahá, *The Promulgation of Universal Peace,* p. 217.

Why is it important to raise a family?

"It is highly important for a man to raise a family. So long as he is young, because of youthful self-complacency, he does not realize its significance, but this will be a source of regret when he grows old." 'Abdu'l-Bahá, in *Lights of Guidance*, no. 733.

What qualities are vital to a family?

"If love and agreement are manifest in a single family, that family will advance, become illumined and spiritual; but if enmity and hatred exist within it, destruction and dispersion are inevitable." 'Abdu'l-Bahá, *The Promulgation of Universal Peace*, p. 200.

". . . the life of a married couple should resemble the life of the angels in heaven—a life full of joy and spiritual delight, a life of unity and concord, a friendship both mental and physical. The home should be orderly and well-organized. Their ideas and thoughts should be like the rays of the sun of truth and the radiance of the brilliant stars in the heavens. Even as two birds they should warble melodies upon the branches of the tree of fellowship and harmony. They should always be elated with joy and gladness and be a source of happiness to the hearts of others. They should set an example to their fellow-men, manifest true and sincere love towards each other and educate their children in such a manner as to blazon the fame and glory of their family." 'Abdu'l-Bahá, in *Lights of Guidance*, no. 733.

How can we solve conflict in a family?

"Bahá'u'lláh also stressed the importance of consultation. We should not think this worthwhile method of seeking solutions is confined to the administrative institutions of the Cause. Family consultation employing full and frank discussion, and animated by awareness of the need for moderation and balance, can be the panacea for domestic conflict." Letter written on behalf of the Universal House of Justice, *The Compilation of Compilations, vol. II,* no. 2160.

Domestic Violence

Is domestic violence ever acceptable?

"Both Bahá'u'lláh and 'Abdu'l-Bahá stressed love and harmony as the hallmark of marriage. Furthermore, in the view of 'Abdu'l-Bahá's exhortation that each member of the family must uphold the rights of the others, makes it clear that violence in the family is contrary to the spirit of the Faith and a practice to be condemned." The Universal House of Justice, *Lights of Guidance,* no. 740.

"[In] the marital relationship, as in all others, mutual consideration and respect should apply. If a Bahá'í woman suffers abuse or is subjected to rape by her husband, she has the right to turn to the Spiritual Assembly for assistance and counsel, or to seek legal protection. Such abuse would gravely jeopardize the continuation of the marriage . . ." The Universal House of Justice, *Letter from the Universal House of Justice, 24 January 1993,* ¶17.

Planning a Family

Is it important for a married couple to have children?

"Bahá'u'lláh explicitly reveals in His Book of Laws that the very purpose of marriage is the procreation of children who, when grown up, will be able to know God and to recognize and observe His Commandments and Laws as revealed through His Messengers. Marriage is thus, according to the Bahá'í Teachings, primarily a social and moral act." Shoghi Effendi, in a letter to an individual believer, *Lights of Guidance* no. 1160.

What about birth control and abortion?

It is up to the husband and wife to decide when to have children and how many. The Bahá'í writings explain that the soul appears at conception and so the birth control they use should not be one that aborts the fetus. In cases of rape or when a pregnancy threatens the life of the mother, Bahá'ís are asked to make a decision based on medical advice, their own consciences, and the general guidance given in the Bahá'í writings. Any surgical procedure that results in permanent sterility is to be avoided unless it is medically necessity.

"Abortion and surgical operations for the purpose of preventing the birth of unwanted children are forbidden in the Cause unless there are circumstances which justify such actions on medical grounds, in which case the decision, at present, is left to the consciences of those concerned who must carefully weigh the medical advice in the light of the general guidance given in the Teachings." The Universal House of Justice, in *Lights of Guidance,* no. 1155.

Raising Children

What are the primary duties of parents?

"Teach ye your children so that they may peruse the divine verses every morn and eve." Bahá'u'lláh, in *The Compilation of Compilations, vol. I,* no. 5.

> It is enjoined upon the father and mother, as a duty, to strive with all effort to train the daughter and the son, to nurse them from the breast of knowledge and to rear them in the bosom of sciences and arts. Should they neglect this matter, they shall be held responsible and worthy of reproach in the presence of the stern Lord. 'Abdu'l-Bahá, *Selections from the Writings of 'Abdu'l-Bahá,* no. 98.2.

> Oh ye loving mothers, know that in God's sight, the best of all ways to worship Him is to educate the children and train them in all the perfections of humankind; and no nobler deed than this can be imagined.
> 'Abdu'l-Bahá, *Selections from the Writings of 'Abdu'l-Bahá,* no 114.1.

Are the duties of mothers and fathers somewhat different?

"God hath prescribed unto every father to educate his children, both boys and girls, in the sciences and in morals, and in crafts and professions." Bahá'u'lláh, in *The Compilation of Compilations, vol. I,* no. 5.

"That the first teacher of the child is the mother should not be startling, for the primary orientation of the infant is to its mother. This provision of nature in no way minimizes the role of the father in the Bahá'í family. . . . equality of status does not mean identity of function." The Universal House of Justice, in *The Compilation of Compilations, vol. II,* no. 2159.

". . . although the mother is the first educator of the child, and the most important formative influence in his development, the father also has the responsibility of educating his children, and this responsibility is so weighty that Bahá'u'lláh has stated that a father who fails to exercise it forfeits his rights of fatherhood." The Universal House of Justice, *Messages from the Universal House of Justice, 1963–1986,* no. 272.6.

". . . the man has primary responsibility for the financial support of the family, and the woman is the chief and primary educator of the children. This by no means implies that these functions are inflexibly fixed and cannot be changed and adjusted to suit particular family situations, nor does it mean that the place of the woman is confined to the home. Rather, while primary responsibility is assigned, it is anticipated that fathers would play a significant role in the education of the children and women could also be breadwinners." The Universal House of Justice, in *Lights of Guidance,* no. 2118.

How do parental roles change with time?

"The great importance attached to the mother's role derives from the fact that she is the first educator of the child. Her attitude, her prayers, even  what she eats and her physical condition have a great influence on the child when it is still in the womb. When the child is born, it is she who has been endowed by God with the milk which is the first food designed for it, and it is intended that, if possible, she should be with the baby to train and nurture it in its earliest days and months. This does not mean that the father does not also love, pray for

and care for his baby, but as he has the primary responsibility of providing for the family, his time to be with his child is usually limited, while the mother is usually closely associated with the baby during this intensely formative time when it is growing and developing faster than it ever will again during the whole of its life. As the child grows older and more independent, the relative nature of its relationship with its mother and father modifies and the father can play a greater role." The Universal House of Justice, *Messages from the Universal House of Justice, 1963–1986,* no. 407.

How should a child be disciplined?

"Let the mothers consider that whatever concerneth the education of children is of the first importance. Let them put forth every effort in this regard, for when the bough is green and tender it will grow in whatever way ye train it. Therefore it is incumbent upon the mothers to rear their little ones even as a gardener tendeth his young plants. Let them strive by day and by night to establish within their children faith and certitude, the fear of God, the love of the Beloved of the worlds, and all good qualities and traits. Whensoever a mother seeth that her child hath done well, let her praise and applaud him and cheer his heart; and if the slightest undesirable trait should manifest itself, let her counsel the child and punish him, and use means based on reason, even a slight verbal chastisement should this be necessary. It is not, however, permissible to strike a child, or vilify him, for the child's character will be totally perverted if he be subjected to blows or verbal abuse." 'Abdu'l-Bahá, *Selections from the Writings of 'Abdu'l-Bahá*, no. 95.2.

Educating Children

"Knowledge is as wings to man's life, and a ladder for his ascent. Its acquisition is incumbent upon everyone." Bahá'u'lláh, Epistle to the Son of the Wolf, p. 26.

Must every child be educated?

". . . in this new cycle, education and training are recorded in the Book of God as obligatory and not voluntary. That is, it is enjoined upon the father and mother, as a duty, to strive with all effort to train the daughter and the son, to nurse them from the breast of knowledge and to rear them in the bosom of sciences and arts. Should they neglect this matter, they shall be held responsible and worthy of reproach in the presence of the stern Lord." 'Abdu'l-Bahá, *Selections from the Writings of 'Abdu'l-Bahá*, no. 98.2.

What if parents are unable to educate their children?

"If the parents are able to provide the expenses of this education, it is alright, otherwise the community must provide the means for the teaching of that child." 'Abdu'l-Bahá, *Selections from the Writings of 'Abdu'l-Bahá*, no. 227.23.

Should everyone in a community contribute financially to the education of children?

"Everyone, whether man or woman, should hand over to a trusted person a portion of what he or she earneth through trade, agriculture or other occupation, for the training and education of children, to be spent for this purpose with the knowledge of the Trustees of the House of Justice." The Universal House of Justice, *Messages from the Universal House of Justice, 1963–1986*, no. 222.13.

What is the value of educating women?

"Furthermore, the education of women is more necessary and important than that of man, for woman is the trainer of the child from its infancy. If she be defective and imperfect herself, the child will necessarily be deficient; therefore, imperfection of woman implies a condition of imperfection in all mankind, for it is the mother who rears, nurtures and guides the growth of the child." 'Abdu'l-Bahá, *Promulgation of Universal Peace,* p. 185.

Should boys and girls receive similar education?

"Bahá'u'lláh hath proclaimed the universality of education, which is essential to the unity of mankind, that one and all may be equally educated, whether girls or boys, and receive the same education. When education is universalized in all schools, perfect communication between the members of the human race will be established. When all receive the same kind of education the foundations of war and contention will be utterly destroyed." 'Abdu'l-Bahá, in *Bahá'í Education,* no. 82.

Is teaching a noble profession?

"Among the greatest of all services that can possibly be rendered by man to Almighty God is the education and training of children. It is, however, very difficult to undertake this service, even harder to succeed in it." 'Abdu'l-Bahá, *Selections from the Writings of 'Abdu'l-Bahá,* no. 106.1.

Which subjects should a child study?

". . . every child must learn reading and writing, and acquire such branches of knowledge as are useful and necessary, as well as learning an art or skill. The utmost care must be devoted to these matters; any neglect of them, any failure to act on them, is not permissible." 'Abdu'l-Bahá, in *The Compilation of Compilations, vol. I,* no. 17.

"Every child without exception must from his earliest years make a thorough study of the art of reading and writing, and according to his own tastes and inclinations and the degree of his capacity and powers, devote extreme diligence to the acquisition of learning beneficial arts and skills, various languages, speech and contemporary technology." Shoghi Effendi, in *The Compilation of Compilations, vol. I,* no. 656.

How should schools be organized?

"Establish schools that are well organized, and promote the fundamentals of instruction in the various branches of knowledge through teachers who are pure and sanctified, distinguished for their high standards of conduct and general excellence, and strong in faith; educators with a thorough knowledge of sciences and arts." 'Abdu'l-Baha, in *The Compilation of Compilations, vol. I,* no. 22.

The Principles of Education

"The universities and colleges of the world must hold fast to three cardinal principles. First: Whole-hearted service to the cause of education, the unfolding of the mysteries of nature, the extension of the boundaries of pure science, the elimination of the causes of ignorance and social evils, a standard universal system of instruction, and the diffusion of the lights of knowledge and reality.

Second: Service to the cause of morality, raising the moral tone of the students, inspiring them with the sublimest ideals of ethical refinement, teaching them altruism, inculcating in their lives the beauty of holiness and the excellency of virtue and animating them with the excellences and perfections of the religion of God.

Third: Service to the oneness of the world of humanity; so that each student may consciously realize that he is a brother to all mankind, irrespective of religion or race. The thoughts of universal peace must be instilled into the minds of all the scholars, in order that they may become the armies of peace, the real servants of the body politic—the world. God is the Father of all. Mankind are His children. This globe is one home. Nations are the members of one family. The mothers in their homes, the teachers in the schools, the professors in the college, the presidents in the universities, must teach these ideals to the young from the cradle up to the age of manhood." 'Abdu'l-Bahá, in "Bahai Methods of Education," *Star of the West*, vol. 9, no. 9, p. 98.

How can education prevent crime?

"Observe how many penal institutions, houses of detention and places of torture are made ready to receive the sons of man, the purpose being to prevent them, by punitive measures, from committing terrible crimes—whereas this very torment and punishment only increaseth depravity. Therefore must the individual be

> Regard man as a mine rich in gems of inestimable value. Education can, alone, cause it to reveal its treasures, and enable mankind to benefit therefrom.
>
> Bahá'u'lláh, *Gleanings from the Writings of Baha'u'llah*, no. 122.1.

trained from his infancy in such a way that he will never undertake to commit a crime, will, rather, direct all his energies to the acquisition of excellence, and will look upon the very commission of an evil deed as in itself the harshest of all punishments, considering the sinful act itself to be far more grievous than any prison sentence. For it is possible so to train the individual that, although crime may not be completely done away with, still it will become very rare." 'Abdu'l-Bahá, in *The Compilation of Compilations, vol. I,* no. 590.

"O God! Educate these children. These children are the plants of Thine orchard, the flowers of Thy meadow, the roses of Thy garden. Let Thy rain fall upon them; let the Sun of Reality shine upon them with Thy love. Let Thy breeze refresh them in order that they may be trained, grow and develop, and appear in the utmost beauty. Thou art the Giver. Thou art the Compassionate." 'Abdu'l-Bahá, *The Promulgation of Universal Peace,* p. 271.

CHAPTER 20

The Water of Life: Laws and Ordinances

> The laws of God are not imposition of will, or of power, or of pleasure, but the resolutions of truth, reason and justice.
>
> 'Abdu'l-Bahá, *Paris Talks,* no. 47.1.

> . . . a new Faith, a new Law, and a new Revelation . . .
>
> Bahá'u'lláh, Kitáb-i-Iqán, ¶268.

The revelation of Bahá'u'lláh is intended to heal the illnesses of modern civilization and foster peace throughout the world. In order to achieve this, His teachings set a high standard for human behavior and require each person to increase his or her understanding of the spiritual nature of physical life. This chapter highlights several laws and principles—and some virtues—that were not covered in previous chapters.

"O ye who are as dead! The Hand of Divine bounty proffereth unto you the Water of Life. Hasten and drink your fill. Whoso hath been reborn in this Day, shall never die; whoso remaineth dead, shall never live." Bahá'u'lláh,

Gleanings from the Writings of Bahá'u'lláh, no. 106.3.

Obeying the Laws of God

"The first duty prescribed by God for His servants is the recognition of Him Who is the Dayspring of His Revelation and the Fountain of His laws, Who representeth the Godhead in both the Kingdom of His Cause and the world of creation. Whoso achieveth this duty hath attained unto all good; and whoso is deprived thereof hath gone astray, though he be the author of every righteous deed. It behooveth every one who reacheth this most sublime station, this summit of transcendent glory, to observe every ordinance of Him Who is the Desire of the world. These twin duties are inseparable. Neither is acceptable without the other. Thus hath it been decreed by Him Who is the Source of Divine inspiration." Bahá'u'lláh, Kitáb-i-Aqdas, ¶1.

Do Messengers of God have the right to change laws of previous religions?

"Were He to decree as lawful the thing which from time immemorial had been forbidden, and forbid that which had, at all times, been regarded as lawful, to none is given the right to question His authority. Whoso will hesitate, though it be for less than a moment, should be regarded as a transgressor." Bahá'u'lláh, Kitáb-i-Aqdas, ¶162.

How do we balance freedom and obedience?

"True liberty consisteth in man's submission unto My commandments, little as ye know it. Were men to observe that which We have sent down unto them from the Heaven of Revelation, they would, of a certainty, attain unto perfect liberty. Happy is the man that hath apprehended the Purpose of God in whatever He hath revealed from the Heaven of His Will, that pervadeth all created things." Bahá'u'lláh, *Gleanings from the Writings of Bahá'u'lláh,* no. 159.4.

Why should we obey laws we don't understand?

"Man often lacks the understanding to fathom the wisdom of some of the ordinances which are not to his liking. It therefore becomes a matter of demonstration of the depth of his faith when he is faced with a divine command the wisdom and rationale of which he cannot at that time understand." The Universal House of Justice, letter to an individual believer, March 3, 1987.

What is the progressive nature of the application of Bahá'í laws?

Just as each Prophet brings teachings suited to the age in which He appears, the laws and teachings of the Prophet are progressively applied within each Dispensation.

Many of Bahá'u'lláh's laws are not yet binding on Bahá'ís the world over. They may be binding in a few countries but not in others because the conditions of certain societies make their application unwise. Or they may not yet be applied anywhere at all because the Bahá'í community is not yet ready for them. The Universal House of Justice is responsible for deciding at what time and in which parts of the world laws that are not already in effect become applicable.

Why did Bahá'u'lláh allow the gradual application of Bahá'í laws?

"Realizing the degree of human frailty, Bahá'u'lláh has provided that other laws are to be applied only gradually, but these too, once they are applied, must be followed, or else society will not be reformed but will sink into an ever worsening condition." The Universal House of Justice, Letter from the Universal House of Justice, February 6, 1973.

What are some examples of laws not yet applied?

Several religious laws that do not conflict with civil law, such as the limit of a ninety-day engagement, some burial requirements, and the giving of a dowry by the groom to the bride have not yet been applied to the Bahá'í community worldwide, although Bahá'ís are free to abide by them as they wish. Various other laws prescribed by Bahá'u'lláh—such as penalties for murder, arson, and other crimes were "formulated in anticipation of a state of society destined to emerge from the chaotic conditions that prevail today" (Intro to the Kitáb-i-Aqdas, p. 6). Therefore, these laws have not yet been applied at any level of society.

What happens when a law is broken?

"There are certain teachings and exhortations [like obligatory prayer] the observance of which is solely between the individual and God; the non-observance of other laws and ordinances incurs some form of sanction. Some of these violations incur punishment for a single offense, while others are punished only after repeated warnings have failed to remedy the violation. It is not possible to establish a single rule applicable automatically and invariably." Letter written on behalf of the Universal House of Justice to an individual believer, February 20, 1977.

Who is responsible for applying sanctions?

Local Spiritual Assemblies are responsible for deciding when and how to deal with violations of Bahá'í law in their communities. They are charged with investigating a situation with the aim of uncovering the facts before taking action and are to consider each case on its own merits. Assemblies often consult with members of the Auxiliary Board and / or the National Spiritual Assembly when judging what to do.

In some cases an Assembly could decide to ignore the behavior for a while, hoping the person will correct it himself. In other situations, it might invite the person to consult with the Assembly about the problem. Assemblies can explain how a situation might be corrected, offer assistance, and / or recommend professional assistance.

In extreme cases when rectification is not possible and a law was broken deliberately, the administrative rights of the individual might be removed. Bahá'ís who have lost these rights can be restricted from participating in community life in certain ways, including being restricted from attending the Nineteen-Day Feast, not be-ing allowed to contribute to the Bahá'í Funds, as well as not being permitted to vote in Bahá'í elections.

How can administrative rights be restored?

Restoration depends on several things, including sincere repentance and demonstrating that the condition has been corrected. The most serious cases are not handled locally but are referred to the Universal House of Justice.

Which violations might incur some form of sanction?

A few examples of sanction-worthy violations are: prolonged use of alcohol or illegal drugs, violation of marriage laws, criminal offenses, physical or sexual abuse, gambling, fraudulent behavior, flagrant immorality, engaging in partisan politics.

The Obligation to Work

"It is made incumbent on each one of you to engage in some occupation, such as a craft, a trade or the like. We have exalted your engagement in such work to the rank of worship of the one true God. Reflect, O people, on the grace and blessings of your Lord, and yield Him thanks at eventide and dawn. Waste not your hours in idleness and sloth, but occupy yourselves with what will profit you and others. Thus hath it been decreed in the Tablet from whose horizon hath shone the daystar of wisdom and utterance. The most despised of men in the sight of God are they who sit and beg. Hold ye fast unto the cord of means and place your trust in God, the Provider of all means." Bahá'u'lláh, Kitáb-i-Aqdas, ¶33.

Does homemaking count as work?

". . . homemaking is a highly honourable and responsible work of fundamental importance for mankind." The Universal House of Justice, in *Lights of Guidance,* no. 2117.

Are women free to work outside the home?

Yes, see chapter 19.

What about the very poor and the very rich?

". . . mendicity (begging) should not only be discouraged but entirely wiped out from the face of society. It is the duty of those who are in charge of the organization of society to give every individual the opportunity of acquiring the necessary talent in some kind of profession, and also the means of utilizing such a talent, both for its own sake and for the sake of earning the means of his livelihood. Every individual, no matter how handicapped and limited he may be, is under the obligation of engaging in some work or profession. . . . It is obvious, therefore, that the inheritance of wealth cannot make anyone immune from daily work." Letter written on behalf of Shoghi Effendi, in *Lights of Guidance,* no. 2106.

Loyalty to Government

"In any country where any of this people (Bahá'ís) reside, they must behave towards the government of that country with loyalty, honesty and truthfulness. This is that which hath been revealed at the behest of Him Who is the Ordainer, the Ancient of Days." Bahá'u'lláh, *Tablets of Bahá'u'lláh,* pp. 22–23.

Gambling

"Gambling and the use of opium have been forbidden unto you. Eschew them both, O people, and be not of those who transgress." Bahá'u'lláh, Kitáb-i-Aqdas, ¶155.

Avoiding Intoxicants

The use of alcohol, marijuana, opium, and similar intoxicants is forbidden, though some of these things may be used medicinally if prescribed by a physician for a specific ailment. The use of tobacco, though strongly discouraged, is not forbidden.

What are some reasons for avoiding mind-altering substances?

"It is inadmissible that man, who hath been endowed with reason, should consume that which stealeth it away. Nay, rather it behooveth him to comport himself in a manner worthy of the human station, and not in accordance with the misdeeds of every heedless and wavering soul." Bahá'u'lláh, Kitáb-i-Aqdas, ¶119.

"Beware of using any substance that induceth sluggishness and torpor in the human temple and inflicteth harm upon the body. We, verily, desire for you naught save what shall profit you, and to this bear witness all created things, had ye but ears to hear." Bahá'u'lláh, Kitáb-i-Aqdas, ¶155.

"Alcohol consumeth the mind and causeth man to commit acts of absurdity, but this opium, this foul fruit of the infernal tree, and this wicked hashish extinguish the mind, freeze the spirit, petrify the soul, waste the body and leave man frustrated and lost." 'Abdu'l-Bahá, cited in the Kitáb-i-Aqdas, note 170, p. 239.

"As to opium, it is foul and accursed. God protect us from the punishment He inflicteth on the user. According to the explicit Text of the Most Holy Book, it is forbidden, and its use is utterly condemned. Reason showeth that smoking opium is a kind of insanity, and experience attesteth that the user is completely cut off from the human kingdom. May God protect all against the perpetration of an act so hideous as this, an act which layeth in ruins the very foundation of what it is to be human, and which causeth the user to be dispossessed for ever and ever. For opium fasteneth on the soul, so that the user's conscience dieth, his mind is blotted away, his perceptions are eroded. It turneth the living into the dead." 'Abdu'l-Bahá, *Selections from the Writings of 'Abdu'l-Bahá,* no. 129.10.

"Regarding hashish [a concentrated preparation made from certain parts of the marajuana plant] . . . Its use causeth the disintegration of thought and the complete torpor of the soul . . . extinguisheth the mind, freezeth the spirit, petrifieth the soul, wasteth the body and leaveth man frustrated and lost." 'Abdu'l-Bahá, cited in Kitáb-i-Aqdas, note 170, p. 239.

Why is smoking discouraged?

"... in the sight of God, smoking tobacco is deprecated, abhorrent, filthy in the extreme; and, albeit by degrees, highly injurious to health. It is also a waste of money and time, and maketh the user a prey to a noxious addiction. To those who stand firm in the Covenant, this habit is therefore censured both by reason and experience, and renouncing it will bring relief and peace of mind to all men." 'Abdu'l-Bahá, *Selections from the Writings of 'Abdu'l-Bahá,* no. 129.9.

Truthfulness

"Truthfulness is the foundation of all human virtues. Without truthfulness, progress and success in all of the worlds of God are impossible for a soul. When this holy attribute is established in man, all the divine qualities will also become realized." 'Abdu'l-Bahá, cited in Shoghi Effendi, *The Advent of Divine Justice,* ¶40.

"Beautify your tongues, O people, with truthfulness, and adorn your souls with the ornament of honesty." Bahá'u'lláh, *Gleanings from the Writings of Bahá'u'lláh,* no. 136.6.

Trustworthiness

"Adorn your heads with the garlands of trustworthiness and fidelity, your hearts with the attire of the fear of God, your tongues with absolute truthfulness, your bodies with the vesture of courtesy. These are in truth seemly adornings unto the temple of man, if ye be of them that reflect." Bahá'u'lláh, Kitáb-i-Aqdas, ¶120.

"Trustworthiness is the greatest portal leading unto the tranquillity and security of the people. In truth the stability of every affair hath depended and doth depend upon it. All the domains of power, of grandeur and of wealth are illumined by its light." Bahá'u'lláh, *Tablets of Bahá'u'lláh,* p. 37.

Kindness to Animals

"Burden not an animal with more than it can bear. We, truly, have prohibited such treatment through a most binding interdiction in the Book. Be ye the embodiments of justice and fairness amidst all creation." Bahá'u'lláh, Kitáb-i-Aqdas, ¶187.

"Train your children from their earliest days to be infinitely tender and loving to animals. If an animal be sick, let the children try to heal it, if it be hungry, let them feed it, if thirsty, let them quench its thirst, if weary, let them see that it rests." 'Abdu'l-Bahá, *Selections from the Writings of Abdu'l-Bahá,* no. 138.4.

Cleanliness

Bahá'u'lláh set minimum standards for cleanliness throughout the world: keeping one's clothes clean, cutting one's nails and bathing (or showering) regularly. He also provided standards for clean water.

"Cleave ye unto the cord of refinement with such tenacity as to allow no trace of dirt to be seen upon your garments. Such is the injunc-

tion of One Who is sanctified above all refinement. Whoso falleth short of this standard with good reason shall incur no blame." Bahá'u'lláh, Kitáb-i-Aqdas, ¶74.

How is cleanliness related to spirituality?
"And although bodily cleanliness is a physical thing, it hath, nevertheless, a powerful influence on the life of the spirit. It is even as a voice wondrously sweet, or a melody played: although sounds are but vibrations in the air which affect the ear's auditory nerve, and these vibrations are but chance phenomena carried along through the air, even so, see how they move the heart. A wondrous melody is wings for the spirit, and maketh the soul to tremble for joy. The purport is that physical cleanliness doth also exert its effect upon the human soul." 'Abdu'l-Bahá, *Selections from the Writings of 'Abdu'l-Bahá*, p. 147.

Food

". . . there is nothing in the teachings about whether people should eat their food cooked or raw; exercise or not exercise; resort to specific therapies or not; nor is it forbidden to eat meat." Shoghi Effendi, in *Lights of Guidance,* no. 1017.

"No specific school of nutrition or medicine has been associated with the Bahá'í teachings. What we have are certain guidelines, indications and principles which will be carefully studied by experts and will, in the years ahead, undoubtedly prove to be invaluable sources of guidance and inspiration in the development of these medical sciences." Letter written on behalf of the Universal House of Justice, in *Lights of Guidance,* no. 1015.

Is a vegetarian diet mentioned in the Bahá'í Writings?

'Abdu'l-Bahá states that when mankind is more spiritually developed, the eating of meat will gradually cease.

"Thou hast written regarding the four canine teeth in man, saying that these teeth, two in the upper jaw and two in the lower, are for the purpose of eating meat. Know thou that these four teeth are not created for meat-eating, although one can eat meat with them. All the teeth of man are made for eating fruit, cereals and vegetables. These four teeth, however, are designed for breaking hard shells, such as those of almonds. But eating meat is not forbidden or unlawful, nay, the point is this, that it is possible for man to live without eating meat and still be strong. Meat is nourishing and containeth the elements of herbs, seeds and fruits; therefore sometimes it is essential for the sick and for the rehabilitation of health. There is no objection in the Law of God to the eating of meat if it is required. So if thy constitution is rather weak and thou findest meat useful, thou mayest eat it." 'Abdu'l-Bahá, in *Lights of Guidance,* no. 1007.

Carrying Arms and Military Service

Carrying arms is forbidden, except under certain circumstances. If one is drafted, military service is permitted but noncombatant status should be sought. If this status is denied, Bahá'ís are to serve as requested by the government.

What about hunting?

Hunting with guns or bow and arrow or other means is not forbidden, though Bahá'u'lláh warns that one should not hunt to excess. He does, however, forbid the eating of game found dead in a trap or net.

Do Bahá'ís ever enlist in the military?

"There is no objection to a Bahá'í's enlisting voluntarily in the armed forces of a country in order to obtain a training in some trade or profession, provided that he can do so without making himself liable to undertake combatant service." Letter from the Universal House of Justice, January 13, 1981.

Writing a Will

"Unto everyone hath been enjoined the writing of a will." Bahá'u'lláh, Kitáb-i-Aqdas, ¶109.

"According to the Teachings of Bahá'u'lláh, the making of a will is essentially an obligation of the individual Bahá'í. Each believer is free to dispose of his estate in whatever manner he chooses, within the limits imposed by civil law and after payment of burial expenses and other debts and obligations. There are several ways a believer can leave instructions regarding his burial; there is no objection for such instructions to be included in the will, if the law permits, and the believer so wishes." Letter written on behalf of The Universal House of Justice, in *Lights of Guidance,* no. 631.

Burial

Burial, not cremation, has been ordained by Bahá'u'lláh. Bahá'í law dictates that the dead should be treated with respect, should not be embalmed unless required by law, and if possible, should be buried no further than one hour's journey from the place of death. Before burial, the Prayer for the Dead is to be said by one believer while those attending stand and listen.

"As this physical frame is the throne of the inner temple, whatever occurs to the former is felt by the latter. In reality that which takes delight in joy or is saddened by pain is the inner temple of the body, not the body itself. Since this physical body is the throne whereon the inner temple is established, God hath ordained that the body be preserved to the extent possible, so that nothing that causeth repugnance may be experienced. The inner temple beholdeth its physical frame, which is its throne. Thus, if the latter is accorded respect, it as if the former is the recipient. The converse is likewise true.

"Therefore, it hath been ordained that the dead body should be treated with the utmost honor and respect." The Báb, *Selections from the Writings of the Báb,* no. 3:23:1–2.

Pilgrimage

A formal visit to the Bahá'í shrines and holy places in 'Akká and Haifa, Israel, for nine days is called a *pilgrimage*. In the future, pilgrimages will include several sites in Iran and Iraq that are not currently accessible due to political constraints. Bahá'u'lláh asks men to make a pilgrimage if they are financially able, while women can choose to go or not.

The schedule is organized by the Pilgrimage Office at the Bahá'í World Center, and application forms are available online or by request.

"Render thanks unto God that thou didst come to the Blessed Spot, didst lay thy head upon the Threshold of the Sacred Shrine, and didst make pilgrimage to the hallowed sanctuary round which circle in adoration the intimates of the spiritual realm." 'Abdu'l-Bahá, in a letter from the Universal House of Justice to National Spiritual Assemblies, dated August 16, 2017.

"You have asked about visiting holy places and the observance of marked reverence toward these resplendent spots. Holy places are undoubtedly centres of the outpouring of Divine grace, because on entering the illumined sites associated with martyrs and holy souls, and by observing reverence, both physical and spiritual, one's heart is moved with great tenderness." 'Abdu'l-Bahá, in *Lights of Guidance,* no. 1828.

"O my Lord and my Hope! Help Thou Thy loved ones to be steadfast in Thy mighty Covenant, to remain faithful to Thy manifest Cause, and to carry out the commandments Thou didst set down for them in Thy Book of Splendors; that they may become banners of guidance and lamps of the Company above, wellsprings of Thine infinite wisdom, and stars that lead aright, as they shine down from the supernal sky.

Verily art Thou the Invincible, the Almighty, the All-Powerful." 'Abdu'l-Bahá, *Selections from the Writings of 'Abdu'l-Bahá,* nos. 206.16–17.

CHAPTER 21

Hope for the Future

"Say, Lo! The Father is come, and that which ye were promised in the Kingdom is fulfilled!"

Bahá'u'lláh, *Tablets of Bahá'u'lláh,* p. 11.

". . . the Dispensation of Bahá'u'lláh—the Ark of human salvation . . ."

Shoghi Effendi, *World Order of Bahá'u'lláh,* p. 19.

What is this stage of human history?

"[Bahá'u'lláh's] mission is to proclaim that the ages of the infancy and of the childhood of the human race are past, that the convulsions associated with the present stage of its adolescence are slowly and painfully preparing it to attain the stage of manhood, and are heralding the approach of that Age of Ages when swords will be beaten into plowshares, when the Kingdom promised by Jesus Christ will have been established, and the peace of the planet definitely and permanently ensured." Shoghi Effendi, *The Promised Day is Come,* ¶ii.

What are some of the ancient promises that are in the process of being fulfilled?

"Our Father, which art in Heaven, Hallowed be thy name. Thy kingdom come, Thy will be done, in earth as it is in heaven." Matthew 6:9–10.

"And it shall come to pass in the last days, that the mountain of the Lord's house shall be established in the top of the mountains, and shall be exalted above the hills; and all nations shall flow unto it.

And many people shall go and say, Come ye, and let us go up to the mountain of the Lord, to the house of the God of Jacob; and he will teach us of his ways, and we will walk in his paths: for out of Zion shall go forth the law, and the word of the Lord from Jerusalem.

And he shall judge among the nations, and shall rebuke many people: and they shall beat their swords into plowshares, and their spears into pruninghooks: nation shall not lift up sword against nation, neither shall they learn war any more." Isaiah 2:2–4.

The Current Turmoil

If peace is coming, why is the world such a mess right now?

The Bahá'í writings explain that the turmoil we are currently experiencing is part of the process of the maturing of the human race. When Bahá'u'lláh appeared, His revelation set into motion two simultaneous processes: the collapse of institutions and traditions that no longer benefit humanity and the rise of new ways of living that will eventually create a culture of justice, unity, and peace. The ultimate outcome is good, but the road there is very bumpy.

"The winds of despair are, alas, blowing from every direction, and the strife that divideth and afflicteth the human race is daily increasing.

The signs of impending convulsions and chaos can now be discerned, inasmuch as the prevailing order appeareth to be lamentably defective." Bahá'u'lláh, *Gleanings from the Writings of Bahá'u'lláh*, no. 110.1.

"The world is wrapped in the thick darkness of open revolt and swept by a whirlwind of hate. It is the fires of malevolence that have cast up their flames to the clouds of heaven, it is a blood-drenched flood that rolleth across the plains and down the hills, and no one on the face of the earth can find any peace." 'Abdu'l-Bahá, *Selections from the Writings of 'Abdu'l-Bahá*, no. 236.5.

"A tempest, unprecedented in its violence, unpredictable in its course, catastrophic in its immediate effects, unimaginably glorious in its ultimate consequences, is at present sweeping the face of the earth. Its driving power is remorselessly gaining in range and momentum. Its cleansing force, however much undetected, is increasing with every passing day. Humanity, gripped in the clutches of its devastating power, is smitten by the evidences of its resistless fury. It can neither perceive its origin, nor probe its significance, nor discern its outcome. Bewildered, agonized and helpless, it watches this great and mighty wind of God invading the remotest and fairest regions of the earth, rocking its foundations, deranging its equilibrium, sundering its nations, disrupting the homes of its peoples, wasting its cities, driving into exile its kings, pulling down its bulwarks, uprooting its institutions, dimming its light, and harrowing up the souls of its inhabitants." Shoghi Effendi, *The Promised Day is Come*, ¶2.

A Time of Tremendous Change

"Soon will the present-day order be rolled up, and a new one spread out in its stead. Verily, thy Lord speaketh the truth, and is the Knower of things unseen." Bahá'u'lláh, *Gleanings from the Writings of Bahá'u'lláh*, no. 4.2.

"The whole earth is now in a state of pregnancy. The day is approaching when it will have yielded its noblest fruits, when from it will have sprung forth the loftiest trees, the most enchanting blossoms, the most heavenly blessings." Bahá'u'lláh, cited in Shoghi Effendi, *The Promised Day is Come*, ¶8.

"The world is, in truth, moving on towards its destiny. The interdependence of the peoples and nations of the earth, whatever the leaders of the divisive forces of the world may say or do, is already an accomplished fact. Its unity in the economic sphere is now understood and recognized. The welfare of the part means the welfare of the whole, and the distress of the part brings distress to the whole. The Revelation of Bahá'u'lláh has, in His own words, 'lent a fresh impulse and set a new direction' to this vast process now operating in the world. The fires lit by this great ordeal are the consequences of men's failure to recognize it. They are, moreover, hastening its consummation. Adversity, prolonged, worldwide, afflictive, allied to chaos and universal destruction, must needs convulse the nations, stir the conscience of the world, disillusion the masses, precipitate a radical change in the very conception of society and coalesce ultimately the disjointed, the bleeding limbs of mankind into one body, single, organically united and indivisible." Shoghi Effendi, *The Promised Day is Come,* ¶300.

Will the world end?

"Whatever suffering and turmoil the years immediately ahead may hold, however dark the immediate circumstances, the Bahá'í community believes that humanity can confront this supreme trial with confidence in its ultimate outcome. Far from signalizing the end of civilization, the convulsive changes towards which humanity is being ever more rapidly impelled will serve to release the 'potentialities inherent in the station of man' and reveal 'the full measure of his destiny on earth, the innate excellence of his reality.'" The Universal House of Justice, *Messages from the Universal House of Justice, 1963–1986,* no. 438.11.

A Gradual Transformation

First, Bahá'u'lláh promises, the nations of the world will succeed in establishing a binding political accord designed to bring an end to war. This is called the *Lesser Peace,* and it will be done without direct influence from the Bahá'í Faith or its adherents.

The second stage of peace involves the gradual transformation of the world's peoples into a united, yet still wonderfully diverse, community. This is referred to as *The Most Great Peace* and will spring from the principles and institutions embedded in Bahá'u'lláh's revelation. It is the goal toward which the Bahá'í community labors, and it will involve the spiritualization of the hearts, minds, and lives of the world's inhabitants.

How is the establishment of the first stage of peace described?

"The Great Being, wishing to reveal the prerequisites of the peace and tranquillity of the world and the advancement of its peoples, hath written: The time must come when the imperative necessity for the holding of a vast, an all-embracing assemblage of men will be universally realized. The rulers and kings of the earth must needs attend it, and, participating in its deliberations, must consider such ways and means as will lay the foundations of the world's Great Peace amongst men. Such a peace demandeth that the Great Powers should resolve, for the sake of the tranquillity of the peoples of the earth, to be fully reconciled among themselves. Should any king take up arms against another, all should unitedly arise and prevent him. If this be done, the nations of the world will no longer require any armaments, except for the purpose of preserving the security of their realms and of maintaining internal order within their territories. This will ensure the peace and composure of every people, government and nation." Bahá'u'lláh, *Gleanings from the Writings of Bahá'u'lláh,* no. 117.1.

"A Supreme Tribunal shall be established by the peoples and Governments of every nation, composed of members elected from each country and Government. The members of this Great Council shall assemble in unity. All disputes of an international character shall be submitted to this Court, its work being to arrange by arbitration everything which otherwise would be a cause of war. The mission of this Tribunal would be to prevent war." 'Abdu'l-Bahá, *Paris Talks,* no. 48.1.

What kinds of things will need to be established by the international council?

"In this all-embracing Pact the limits and frontiers of each and every nation should be clearly fixed, the principles underlying the relations of governments towards one another definitely laid down, and all international agreements and obligations ascertained. In like manner, the size of the armaments of every government should be strictly limited, for if the preparations for war and the military forces of any nation should be allowed to increase, they will arouse the suspicion of others. The fundamental principle underlying this solemn Pact should be so fixed that if any government later violate any one of its provisions, all the governments on earth should arise to reduce it to utter submission, nay the human race as a whole should resolve, with every power at its disposal, to destroy that government. Should this greatest of all remedies be applied to the sick body of the world, it will assuredly recover from its ills and will remain eternally safe and secure." 'Abdu'l-Bahá, *The Secret of Divine Civilization,* ¶120.

Will the world realize why all this has happened?

". . . the nations of the earth, as yet unconscious of His Revelation and yet unwittingly enforcing the general principles which He has enunciated, will themselves establish [the Lesser Peace]." Shoghi Effendi, *The Promised Day is Come,* ¶301.

Is the lesser peace a single event or a process?

Bahá'ís generally see it as a process brought about step-by-step. Notable parts of this process possibly include the International Peace Conference held at the Hague in 1899, the establishment of the League of Nations in 1919, the formation of the United Nations at the end of World War II, and, today, the emergence of innumerable organizations, charities, and individual efforts aimed at improving the welfare of diverse peoples, cultivating cooperative projects among far-flung nations, and fostering harmony among different religions.

What principles and institutions have been revealed by Bahá'u'lláh that are necessary for this stage of civilization?

"Bahá'u'lláh, the Sun of Truth, has dawned from the horizon of the Orient, flooding all regions with the light and life which will never pass away. His teachings, which embody the divine spirit of the age and are applicable to this period of maturity in the life of the human world, are:

- The oneness of the world of humanity
- The protection and guidance of the Holy Spirit
- The foundation of all religion is one

- Religion must be the cause of unity
- Religion must accord with science and reason
- Independent investigation of truth
- Equality between men and women
- The abandoning of all prejudices among mankind
- Universal peace
- Universal education
- A universal language
- Solution of the economic problem
- An international tribunal." 'Abdu'l-Bahá, *The Promulgation of Universal Peace,* pp. 619–20.

In the 1930s, Shoghi Effendi outlined Bahá'u'lláh's vision of a peaceful global society. The full text is below, but the spacing has been changed and dots added to highlight each element of this historic description.

"The unity of the human race, as envisaged by Bahá'u'lláh, implies

- the establishment of a world commonwealth in which all nations, races, creeds and classes are closely and permanently united,
- and in which the autonomy of its state members and the personal freedom and initiative of the individuals that compose them are definitely and completely safeguarded.

- This world commonwealth must, as far as we can visualize it, consist of a world legislature, whose members will, as the trustees of the whole of mankind, ultimately control the entire resources of all the component nations, and will enact such laws as shall be required to regulate the life, satisfy the needs and adjust the relationships of all races and peoples.
- A world executive, backed by an international Force, will carry out the decisions arrived at, and apply the laws enacted by this world legislature, and will safeguard the organic unity of the whole commonwealth.
- A world tribunal will adjudicate and deliver its compulsory and final verdict in all and any disputes that may arise between the various elements constituting this universal system.
- A mechanism of world inter-communication will be devised, embracing the whole planet, freed from national hindrances and restrictions, and functioning with marvelous swiftness and perfect regularity.
- A world metropolis will act as the nerve center of a world civilization, the focus toward which the unifying forces of life will converge and from which its energizing influences will radiate.
- A world language will either be invented or chosen from among the existing languages

and will be taught in the schools of all the federated nations as an auxiliary language to their mother tongue.

- A world script, a world literature, a uniform and universal system of currency, of weights and measures, will simplify and facilitate intercourse and understanding among the nations and races of mankind.

- In such a world society, science and religion, the two most potent forces in human life, will be reconciled, will cooperate, and will harmoniously develop.

- The press will, under such a system, while giving full scope to the expression of the diversified views and convictions of mankind, cease to be mischievously manipulated by vested interests, whether private or public, and will be liberated from the influence of contending governments and peoples.

- The economic resources of the world will be tapped and fully utilized, the markets will be coordinated and developed, and the distribution of its products will be equitably regulated.

- National rivalries, hatreds and intrigues will cease, and racial animosity and prejudice will be replaced by racial amity, understanding and cooperation.

- The causes of religious strife will be permanently removed,

- economic barriers and restrictions will be completely abolished, and the inordinate distinction between classes will be obliterated. Destitution on the one hand, and gross accumulation of ownership on the other, will disappear.

- The enormous energy dissipated and wasted on war, whether economic or political, will be consecrated
  - to such ends as will extend the range of human inventions and technical development,
  - to the increase of the productivity of mankind,
  - to the extermination of disease,
  - to the extension of scientific research,
  - to the raising of the standard of physical health,
  - to the sharpening and refinement of the human brain,
  - to the exploitation of the unused and unsuspected resources of the planet,
  - to the prolongation of human life, and
- to the furtherance of any other agency that can stimulate the intellectual, the moral, and spiritual life of the entire human race.

- A world federal system, ruling the whole earth and exercising unchallengeable authority over its unimaginably vast resources, blending and embodying the ideals of both the East and West, liberated from the curse of war and its miseries, and bent on the exploitation of all the available sources of energy on the surface of the planet,

- a system in which Force is made the servant of Justice, whose life is sustained by its universal recognition of one God and by its allegiance to one common Revelation— such is the goal towards which humanity, impelled by the unifying forces of life, is moving." Shoghi Effendi, *World Order of Bahá'u'lláh,* pp. 203–04 [bullet points added].

"O Thou kind Lord! Thou hast created all humanity from the same stock. Thou hast decreed that all shall belong to the same household. In Thy Holy Presence they are all Thy servants, and all mankind are sheltered beneath Thy Tabernacle; all have gathered together at Thy Table of Bounty; all are illumined through the light of Thy Providence.

O God! Thou art kind to all, Thou hast provided for all, dost shelter all, conferrest life upon all. Thou hast endowed each and all with talents and faculties, and all are submerged in the Ocean of Thy Mercy.

O Thou kind Lord! Unite all. Let the religions agree and make the nations one, so that they may see each other as one family and the whole earth as one home. May they all live together in perfect harmony.

O God! Raise aloft the banner of the oneness of mankind.

O God! Establish the Most Great Peace.

Cement Thou, O God, the hearts together.

O Thou kind Father, God! Gladden our hearts through the fragrance of Thy love. Brighten our eyes through the Light of Thy Guidance. Delight our ears with the melody of Thy Word, and shelter us all in the Stronghold of Thy Providence. Thou art the Mighty and Powerful, Thou art the Forgiving and Thou art the One Who overlooketh the shortcomings of all mankind." 'Abdu'l-Bahá, *The Promulgation of Universal Peace,* p. 138.

"The Great Being saith: The heaven of divine wisdom is illumined with the two luminaries of consultation and compassion. Take ye counsel together in all matters, inasmuch as consultation is the lamp of guidance which leadeth the way, and is the bestower of understanding." Bahá'u'lláh, *Tablets of Bahá'u'lláh,* p. 168.

"The Great Being saith: O well-beloved ones! The tabernacle of unity hath been raised; regard ye not one another as strangers. Ye are the fruits of one tree, and the leaves of one branch.

We cherish the hope that the light of justice may shine upon the world and sanctify it from tyranny. If the rulers and kings of the earth, the symbols of the power of God, exalted be His glory, arise and resolve to dedicate themselves to whatever will promote the highest interests of the whole of humanity, the reign of justice will assuredly be established amongst the children of men, and the effulgence of its light will envelop the whole earth." Bahá'u'lláh, *Tablets of Bahá'u'lláh,* p. 164.

CHAPTER 22

Joining the Bahá'í Faith

> Thy Paradise is My love; thy heavenly home, reunion with Me. Enter therein and tarry not.
>
> Bahá'u'lláh, Hidden Words, Arabic, no. 6.

If all religions are from the same God, why would anyone change religions?

When a new Messenger comes with a fresh revelation from God, the teachings He brings are tailored precisely to the needs of that age. We can compare this to a high school teacher whose lessons are appropriate for his students but wouldn't be suited to children still in elementary school or to PhD candidates.

People join the Bahá'í Faith because they recognize that Bahá'u'lláh is the divine Teacher Whose lessons are the ones meant for this stage of human evolution. His revelation provides the spiritual nourishment needed by each soul and establishes the foundation for a joyful global civilization.

What are ways to learn more about the Bahá'í Faith?

Most of the Bahá'í communities around the world offer informal introductions to the Bahá'í Faith, called firesides. Firesides are usually held in someone's home and provide a friendly, informal way to ask questions and discuss spiritual topics. There are also more structured courses known as study circles. These meetings are open to everyone and allow people from all walks of life to consider the teachings of Bahá'u'lláh as they apply to their individual and collective lives. The first course for most study circles centers around a workbook that begins with a section on learning how to understand the Bahá'í writings and then moves on to a consideration of prayer. The final section concentrates on life after death.

In addition to firesides and study circles, communities offer classes for children and junior youth as well as high school students. If there are no Bahá'ís in the area where you live, check out the online resources in Appendix B. It might also be fruitful to visit a regional summer or winter school and get to know a few Bahá'ís while studying various aspects of the Bahá'í Faith. In the United States, simply call 1-800-22-UNITE (1-800-228-6483) for free literature and a referral to the nearest Bahá'í community.

If I join the Bahá'í Faith, am I rejecting my previous religion?

Not at all. Just as we cherish our parents or remember with great tenderness a wise teacher we had in elementary school, Bahá'ís revere the previous Messengers of God, respect the religions founded on Their teachings, and admire the spiritual qualities evidenced by Their followers.

How does someone join the Bahá'í Faith?

Enrollment processes vary a little from country to country. In the United States, when a person accepts Bahá'u'lláh as the most recent Manifestation of God and wants to become a member of the American Bahá'í community, he or she either registers online at http://www.bahái.us or signs a card supplied by local Bahá'ís. If registration is done online, the person will be contacted to confirm the decision, and then the nearest Local Spiritual Assembly will be contacted so that the new member can be welcomed.

New Bahá'ís will receive a membership card and will be added to the mailing list to receive the national magazine, *The American Bahá'í*.

There are no rituals surrounding the act of joining the Bahá'í Faith, though some communities may choose to say prayers with the new Bahá'í or have a party or create some other celebratory occasion.

A person who joins as a member of the Bahá'í Faith immediately becomes part of the local Bahá'í community and may begin attending the Nineteen-Day Feast before receiving a membership card. He or she is also eligible to vote and to be elected to serve on an administrative body.

"Render thanks unto the Almighty, and magnify His name, inasmuch as He hath aided thee to recognize a Cause that hath made the hearts of the inhabitants of the heavens and of the earth to tremble, that hath caused the denizens of the Kingdoms of creation and of Revelation to cry out, and through which the hidden secrets of men's breasts have been searched out and tested."

Bahá'u'lláh, *Gleanings from the Writings of Bahá'u'lláh,* no. 135.2.

How does someone resign from membership?

A letter of withdrawal stating that one no longer believes in Bahá'u'lláh should be written either to one's Local Spiritual Assembly or to the National Spiritual Assembly. Bahá'ís believe in the independent investigation of truth and know it is important to honor and respect each person's spiritual decisions. Friends one has made while a member of the Bahá'í Faith should remain friends.

What happens with my children if I become a Bahá'í?

Children of Bahá'í parents are welcome to take part in all Bahá'í activities until they are fifteen years old, at which point they can decide what their spiritual path will be. Children under fifteen are welcome, no matter their religious background, to have their parents register them as Bahá'ís. They may also register themselves with the consent of a parent. If one parent is a Bahá'í and the other is not, the parents consult together to determine what kind of spiritual education they want for their children.

What kind of spiritual growth can be expected after becoming a Bahá'í?

"When a person becomes a Bahá'í, actually what takes place is that the seed of the spirit starts to grow in the human soul. This seed must be watered by the outpourings of the Holy Spirit. These gifts of the spirit are received through prayer, meditation, study of the Holy Utterances and service to the Cause of God. The fact of the matter is that service in the Cause is like the plough which ploughs the physical soil when seeds are sown. It is necessary that the soil be ploughed up, so that it can be enriched, and thus cause a stronger growth of the seed. In exactly the same way the evolution of the spirit takes place through ploughing up the soil of the heart so that it is a constant reflection of the Holy Spirit. In this way the human spirit grows and develops by leaps and bounds.

Naturally there will be periods of distress and difficulty, and even severe tests; but if that person turns firmly towards the Divine Manifestation, studies carefully His Spiritual teachings and receives the blessings of the Holy Spirit, he will find that in reality these tests and difficulties have been the gifts of God to enable him to grow and develop." Letter written on behalf of Shoghi Effendi, in *Lights of Guidance,* no. 247.

Every created thing in the whole universe is but a door leading into His knowledge, a sign of His sovereignty, a revelation of His names, a symbol of His majesty, a token of His power, a means of admittance into His straight Path . . .

Bahá'u'lláh, *Gleanings from the Writings of Bahá'u'lláh,* no. 82.5.

APPENDIX A

Building a Bahá'í Library

There are an incredible number of books about the Bahá'í Faith, from sacred scripture to commentaries and history. The good news for your budget is that free digital versions of many of the books by Bahá'u'lláh, 'Abdu'l-Bahá, and Shoghi Effendi are available as e-books or audio books at http://bahaibookstore.com. Naturally, there are hard copies for sale as well. Here are several lists of books that are the basic building blocks of any personal library.

A Compilation of Bahá'í Prayers

- *Bahá'í Prayers*—Contains dozens of prayers that were revealed by the Báb, Bahá'u'lláh, and 'Abdu'l-Bahá, including the obligatory prayers.

Books by Bahá'u'lláh

Three titles you may consider starting with are:

- *Gleanings from the Writings of Bahá'u'lláh*
- *The Hidden Words*
- *The Kitáb-i-Íqán: The Book of Certitude*

You may also want to add some or all of these:

- *Prayers and Meditations*
- *The Seven Valleys and the Four Valleys*
- *The Summons of the Lord of Hosts*
- *Epistle to the Son of the Wolf*
- *The Kitáb-i-Aqdas: The Most Holy Book*
- *Fountain of Wisdom: A Collection of Writings from Bahá'u'lláh* (also titled *Tablets of Bahá'u'lláh Revealed after the Kitáb-i-Aqdas*)

Books by 'Abdu'l-Bahá

- *Some Answered Questions,* by 'Abdu'l-Bahá—Described by Shoghi Effendi as a book that is extremely important for the study of the Bahá'í Faith. It addresses topics ranging from the nature of life and the condition of man to many Biblical subjects.

- *Selections from the Writings of 'Abdu'l-Bahá*—This is an illuminating collection of the writings of 'Abdu'l-Bahá that covers a medley of topics from the education of children to the unity of mankind, the need for spiritual perfections, and the importance of sacrifice.

- *Paris Talks: Addresses Given by 'Abdu'l-Bahá in 1911*—This book contains the wonderful public addresses delivered by 'Abdu'l-Bahá in Paris in 1911. Topics include the nature of humankind, the soul, the Prophets of God, the purpose of religion, the eventual establishment of world peace, prejudice, the equality of men and women, science and religion, and more.

Books by Shoghi Effendi

- *The World Order of Bahá'u'lláh*—This collection of seven long letters is the gateway to understanding the immense changes taking place in the world as a result of the gradual establishment of Bahá'u'lláh's World Order. It also contains a letter known as "The Dispensation of Bahá'u'lláh," which explains the stations of the Báb, Bahá'u'lláh, and 'Abdu'l-Bahá, as well as the purpose and function of the Bahá'í Administrative Order.

- *God Passes By*—This book covers the history of the first 100 years of the Bahá'í Faith. It also outlines major writings of Bahá'u'lláh, 'Abdu'l-Bahá, and Shoghi Effendi, which makes it a valuable study tool.

Internet Resources

https://www.bahai.org

The official international site of the Bahá'ís of the world. It contains links to articles about the Bahá'í Faith and to numerous other sites, making it a great place to learn more.

https://www.bahai.us

The official site for the Bahá'ís of the United States with information about the Bahá'í Faith and the Bahá'í House of Worship in Wilmette, Illinois. There are also stories, lists of events, ways to request free information, receive free e-newsletters, or arrange to talk with a Bahá'í by phone or video chat.

https://www.bahai.org/library

This searchable site contains an enormous selection of the writings of the Bahá'í Faith in English, Persian, and Arabic.

http://reference.bahai.org/library

This searchable site provides an enormous selection of the writings of the Bahá'í Faith in English, Persian, and Arabic.

https://www.bahaibookstore.com

This is the website for the Bahá'í Bookstore in the United States. It offers free digital downloads of many e-books and audio books, regardless of whether you live in this country.

http://bahainyc.org/
https://bahai.org.sg

Wondering about the activities of a large Bahá'í community? These are the websites of the New York City and Singapore Bahá'í communities. Find out what other Bahá'í communities around the world are doing by searching for "Bahá'ís of" followed by the name of the country or city.

YouTube Channels

These channels have a generous selection of documentaries, lectures, and performances by Bahá'í musicians.

UK Bahá'í Office of Public Affairs

https://www.youtube.com/channel/UCr9YO_pec1WBvQwhanndydQ

The Bahá'í Faith Channel

https://www.youtube.com/channel/UCDjRcNAel02lnZbhchjTcsQ

Bahá'ís of the United States

https://www.youtube.com/user/BahaiNationalCenter

Bahá'í on Air (from New Zealand)

https://www.youtube.com/user/Bahaionair/videos?disable_polymer=1

Bahá'í Blog Studio Sessions

https://www.youtube.com/channel/UC_wNlQnJNP8LRAhjGF3ZLKA

Bibliography

Works of Bahá'u'lláh

Epistle to the Son of the Wolf. Wilmette, IL: Bahá'í Publishing Trust, 1988.

Gleanings from the Writings of Bahá'u'lláh. Wilmette, IL: Bahá'í Publishing, 2005.

The Hidden Words. Translated by Shoghi Effendi. Wilmette, IL: Bahá'í Publishing, 2002.

The Kitáb-i-Aqdas: The Most Holy Book. 1st ps ed. Wilmette, IL: Bahá'í Publishing Trust, 1993.

The Kitáb-i-Íqán: The Book of Certitude. Translated by Shoghi Effendi. Wilmette, IL: Bahá'í Publishing, 2003.

Prayers and Meditations by Bahá'u'lláh. Translated by Shoghi Effendi. 1st ps ed. Wilmette, IL: Bahá'í Publishing Trust, 1987.

The Summons of the Lord of Hosts. Wilmette, IL: Bahá'í Publishing, 2006.

Tablets of Bahá'u'lláh revealed after the Kitáb-i-Aqdas. Compiled by the Research Department of the Universal House of Justice. Translated by Habib Taherzadeh et al. Wilmette, IL: Bahá'í Publishing Trust, 1988.

Works of the Báb

Selections from the Writings of the Báb. Compiled by the Research Department of the Universal House of Justice. Translated by Habib Taherzadeh et al. Wilmette, IL: Bahá'í Publishing Trust, 2006.

Works of 'Abdu'l-Bahá

'Abdu'l-Bahá in London: Addresses & Notes of Conversations. London: Bahá'í Publishing Trust, 1987.

Foundations of World Unity. Wilmette, IL: Bahá'í Publishing Trust, 1972.

Paris Talks: Addresses Given by 'Abdu'l-Bahá in 1911. Wilmette, IL: Bahá'í Publishing, 2011.

The Promulgation of Universal Peace: Talks Delivered by 'Abdu'l-Bahá during His Visit to the United States and Canada in 1912. Wilmette, IL: Bahá'í Publishing, 2012.

The Secret of Divine Civilization. Translated from the Persian by Marzieh Gail in consultation with Ali-Kuli Khan. Wilmette, IL: Bahá'í Publishing, 2007.

Selections from the Writings of Abdu'l-Bahá. Wilmette, IL: Bahá'í Publishing, 2010.

Some Answered Questions. Newly revised by a committee at the Bahá'í World Center. Wilmette, IL: Bahá'í Publishing, 2016.

Tablets of the Divine Plan. 1st pocket-sized ed. Wilmette, IL: Bahá'í Publishing Trust, 1993.

Will and Testament of 'Abdu'l-Bahá. Wilmette, IL: Bahá'í Publishing Trust, 1944.

Works of Shoghi Effendi

The Advent of Divine Justice. Wilmette, IL: Bahá'í Publishing Trust, 2006.

Bahá'í Administration: Selected Messages, 1922–1932. Wilmette, IL: Bahá'í Publishing Trust, 1998.

Dawn of a New Day. Delhi: Bahá'í Publishing Trust, 1970.

Directives from the Guardian. New Delhi: Bahá'í Publishing Trust.

God Passes By. Wilmette, IL: Bahá'í Publishing Trust, 1974.

Letters from the Guardian to Australia and New Zealand 1923–1957. Sydney: Halstead Press, 1970.

Messages to Canada. Thornhill, Ontario: Bahá'í Canada Publications, 1965.

The Promised Day is Come. 1st pocket-sized ed. Wilmette, IL: Bahá'í Publishing Trust, 1996.

The World Order of Bahá'u'lláh. First pocket-sized edition. Wilmette, IL: Bahá'í Publishing Trust, 1991.

Works of the Universal House of Justice

Individual Rights and Freedoms in the World Order of Bahá'u'lláh. Wilmette, IL: Bahá'í Publishing Trust, 1989.

Messages from The Universal House of Justice, 1968–1973. Wilmette, IL: Bahá'í Publishing Trust, 1976.

Messages from the Universal House of Justice, 1963–1986. Wilmette, IL: Bahá'í Publishing Trust, 1996.

The Promise of World Peace: to the Peoples of the World. Wilmette, IL: Bahá'í Publishing Trust, 1985.

Compilations

Bahá'í Education: A compilation of extracts from the Bahá'í Writings. London: Bahá'í Publishing Trust, 1987.

Bahá'í Prayers: A Selection of Prayers Revealed by Bahá'u'lláh, the Báb, and 'Abdu'l-Bahá. Wilmette, IL: Bahá'í Publishing Trust, 2002.

The Compilation of Compilations, vol. I. Victoria, Australia: Bahá'í Publications Australia, 1991.

The Compilation of Compilations, vol. II. Victoria, Australia: Bahá'í Publications Australia, 1991.

Huqúqu'lláh: The Right of God. Nottingham, UK: Bahá'í Publishing Trust, 1986.

Lights of Guidance: A Bahá'í Reference File. Compiled by Helen Hornby. New Delhi, India: Bahá'í Publishing Trust, 1988.

The Nineteen Day Feast. Compiled by the Research Department of the Universal House of Justice. Mona Vale, N. S.W.: National Spiritual Assembly of the Bahá'ís of Australia, 1989.

The Power of Unity: Beyond Prejudice and Racism. Compiled by Bonnie J. Taylor. Wilmette, IL: 1986.

Principles of Bahá'í Administration: A Compilation. Norwich, UK: Fletcher and Son LTD, 1976.

Unrestrained as the Wind. Wilmette, IL: Bahá'í Publishing Trust, 2008.

Other

A Traveller's Narrative. Preface by Edward G. Browne. New York: Bahá'í Publishing Committee, 1930.

The Bahá'ís: A Profile of the Bahá'í Faith and Its Worldwide Community, by the Bahá'í International Community. London: Bahá'í Publishing Trust, 1994.

Balyuzi, H. M. *'Abdu'l-Bahá: The Centre of the Covenant of Bahá'u'lláh*. Oxford: George Ronald, 1987.

Balyuzi, H. M. *Edward Granville Browne and the Bahá'í Faith*. Oxford: George Ronald, 1996.

Nabíl-i-A'zam [Muḥammad-i-Zarandí]. *The Dawn-Breakers: Nabíl's Narrative of the Early Days of the Bahá'í Revelation*. Translated and edited by Shoghi Effendi. Wilmette, IL: Bahá'í Publishing Trust, 1932.

Esslemont, J. E. *Bahá'u'lláh and the New Era: An Introduction to the Bahá'í Faith*. Wilmette, IL Bahá'í Publishing, 2006.

The Holy Bible: Containing the Old and New Testaments, authorized King James Version. New York: Oxford University Press.

Rabbani, Rúḥíyyih. *The Priceless Pearl*. Rutland, UK: Bahá'í Publishing, 2006.

Smith, Melanie, and Paul Lample. *Youth Can Move the World*. Riviera Beach, FL: Palabra Publications, 1991.

Taherzadeh, Adib. *The Covenant of Bahá'u'lláh*. Oxford: George Ronald, 1992.

Walbridge, John. *Sacred Acts, Sacred Space, Sacred Time*. Oxford: George Ronald, 1996.

Index